Becoming

DR. PETER J. MORRY

ISBN: 979-8-89031-291-4 (sc)
ISBN: 979-8-89031-292-1 (hc)
ISBN: 979-8-89031-293-8 (e)

One Galleria Blvd., Suite 1900, Metairie, LA 70001
1-888-421-2397

CONTENTS

PROLOGUE

This book is a journey of discovery; discovery of our world, our universe, of others but most important it is about discovery of self. This book is transformative, and is about experiencing growth in the pursuit of truth and love. This book provides the key to becoming something better; someone better. The best thing about becoming is that the journey is as endless as the potential for growth itself. The joy in life is not in the discovery of the truth for we will never really know what truth is. The joy in life is in the search for truth. There is nothing else. There is no need for anything else.

Because this book is deeply personal, I had second thoughts about publishing it, partly out of a deep respect for all published authors and some nagging self doubts with regards to the worth of my story as it is the product of a lifetime of experience punctuated with mistakes. Yet, I have learned from my mistakes and experienced the healing that learning brings and wish to share it.

Written over a period of forty years my poetry was originally for personal purposes only. It is partly the realization that we are not unique in our fallibility or pain, which has prompted me to share my poetry and stories with others, with the hope that it may have some meaning in another's life. I have a profound respect for my fellow man and have learned enough to know that what separates us as people is miniscule in comparison to what makes us the same. We all think the same thoughts; share the same fears and desires and all want to make a difference. This book will challenge your core values. It will, I hope it will be part of your becoming.

Peter Emma Sailboat

LITTLE PACKETS OF TIME

Everywhere the pulses of Time resonate around me. Rhythms of life, overlapping, interacting, sometimes briefly, sometimes intertwining, sometimes alone.

As I near the end of my brief moment in the river of time I wonder how my crossings have affected the rhythms of others, as we hurry along to our inevitable transformation, mere droplets of energy, bundled together by some unknown and little understood force, heading somewhere. We are "Little Packets of Time" seeking comfort, trying to understand why, and hoping that our journey through the cosmos has meant something, to someone, somewhere.

Sometimes just being is enough. But being has no meaning alone. Neither is it enough to be an observer, or a rider, or a taker, or a user, for there is no joy there.

My brief nanosecond since creation really has little meaning in the macrocosmic universe, except to those that resonate with me in my little packet of time.

My microcosm, small though it be, is filled with beauty all around. If I can: create a smile, touch a heart, wipe a tear, share a care, help a hand, create some joy, love somebody, my journey will light the universe.

Chapter I

BECOMING

I t was a hectic day at work. The news was all bad. The stock markets were crashing. He wanted to forget all the bad news of the day. Bill Meadows had travelled the world, but now he needed sanctuary; he needed to get home to Ferryland, his connection to the Cosmos. He boarded the plane in Toronto International Airport headed for St John's, Newfoundland and eventually after a one hour drive he would be home to his sanctuary in Ferryland.

For over 200 years his family had called Ferryland home. Originally they had come from Portsmouth England in the mid seventeen hundreds. He had been a world traveler but there was no place like Ferryland. He would die happily only there. He loved this magical spot, where waves spawned over 2000 miles away near England would rend themselves in a thunderous outpouring of energy on the rocky reefs that almost reached his house. The sounds, smells, crystal rockets of exploding waves filled his soul with a sense of wonder, drowning even the greatest of his worries, in an ocean of symphonies. Here he could forget everything. A walk on the shore would renew his spirit.

As the plane flew through the night sky Bill was deep in thought. For several years he had been ahead of the curve. His reading had warned of a cataclysmic economic collapse. Few believed it in the beginning. His, like many others were voices in the wilderness. Now the voices were many and louder, the army of believers was growing, but would it be too little too late. The forces against them were overwhelming. What was needed was not only a complete global transformation of society but a deep fundamental change in the thinking of man himself on a global scale. The problem was so immense that he could not seem to get his head around it.

He had been warning for years about the impending crash and because of his insight had been invited to attend an emergency conference being held at the UN in New York. For weeks he had been meeting with philosophers, psychologists, scholars, economists, bankers, politicians, and religious leaders, in a worldwide economic symposium and little had been achieved. Despite the urgency of the situation, and the need for cooperation the participants acted more like combatants and had difficulty getting past the "us versus them" mentality. Many voices were raised but few were heard. They did not realize that the fundamental problem existed not outside but inside of themselves.

The fundamental problem was greed. Accumulation of wealth and power had been a pillar of societies worldwide and had been so for millennia. Changing this core value, a vital ingredient of the cooperation that would be necessary, would be nearly impossible. People still did not realize that to find solutions they were going to have to make an enormous shift in focus and become introspective. A cooling off period had been called for and everyone was sent home and advised to rethink their positions. The conference would reconvene in two weeks and if an agreement could not be reached the world would be plunged into a depression that would most likely last forty years. If a crash occurred some leading economists were predicting hyperinflation at 50% a year for at least five years. In other words, a dollar today would be worth 3 cents five years from now. No one wanted to believe this scenario but the economists were certain that their projections were real. With so much at stake Bill was astounded that people remained intransigent and uncompromising. A recipe that he concluded would lead only to disaster.

His journey from New York to St John's went quickly because of the depth of his concentration on the serious problems of the day. Finally he was home in Ferryland and now he would be able to renew his spirit.

For him Ferryland was not only home but had for his whole life been his umbilical cord. He was born here, he grew up here and he would die here. For years he had travelled the world and never felt as much in touch with nature, God and himself as here. This was his sanctuary. Exhausted he decided to go to bed. Tomorrow he would attack the daunting problems that at this point seemed insurmountable. The entire world would have to come to an agreement on redistribution of wealth and resources. The rich would have to help the poor. The *haves would have to help the have—not's* at a time when everyone was in danger of losing everything. He reflected back sixty plus years when India was being partitioned and Hindu's and Muslims were killing each other in the streets. Then one man, Mahatma Gandhi went on a hunger strike and vowed not to eat one bite until the violence stopped in the entire country of 700 plus million people. For three plus weeks, thousands of people were murdered as Muslims and Hindu became segregated into the modern countries of India and Pakistan. Finally when Gandhi was near death, the violence miraculously stopped out of respect for the great man.

Tomorrow another miracle would be needed. Bill doubted that a leader of that magnitude would ever walk the face of the earth again. He knew that truth and love were powerful weapons. He only hoped that wisdom would eventually triumph over greed. Exhausted, he fell asleep and awoke just before dawn. He watched the sun rise over Goose Island. A glorious day had been forecasted. An early morning walk along the beach would clear his head. He stopped to rest at his special place, a large flat rock at the water's edge he called his Energy rock, the place that for him was simply magical. A large solitary rock with a sloping flat top had been isolated by the erosion of the waves crashing all around it. Laying on this rock perched in the middle of a reef he could escape the bounds of earth. He had at times gone there intending to stay for thirty minutes or so and became so entranced by the magic of the spot, that 30 minutes became five hours.

Laying there Bill recalled an out of body experience he had had as a young man in Churchill Falls Labrador, while working on the project. At the time the project was just begun and the falls and environs were still in a pristine state. He had to hike into the falls from his base camp. He arrived at about 8:00 am and sat on a rock at the top of the falls. The rushing water roared as it lost its supporting bed and crashed at freefall speed into the rocks below only to be catapulted hundreds of feet skyward bursting into rockets of crystal energy transformed into a fine mist that blanketed the surrounding forest. It was magical. It was there that he had his first out of body experience. When Bill arrived it had been 8:00 am. The whole scene; mist, solitude, thunder, were surreal and transforming. He sat down enchanted by the rawness of nature. He was transfixed, when he next looked at his watch it was 10:00 PM. He had been entranced for fourteen hours! Completely unaware of the boundaries of time and gravity, he had soared above the falls, and had seen himself sitting there. He had visited the bald eagles nest. He had felt the spirit of the thousands of natives that flew there with him. When he awoke from his trance he had discovered that it was nearly dark. He also realized that despite sitting perfectly still in an area of the world which was famous for its black flies and mosquitoes he had not one single bite on him. He had become one with the cosmos.

Bill arrived at what he called his energy rock, a place which facilitated meditation and dreaming. As he lay there his thoughts returned to the events of his economic conference. The sixteen leading nations of the world were in disharmony on many major issues. Somehow they had to find a perfect balance on all these issues. The balance had to be perfect or it would not work. Societies were so complex these days it was frustrating. He wondered if it was so in the dawn of man, when societies were just forming and man was in closer contact with nature. Things must have been simpler then.

He could think clearly on this rock. It was his favorite place to go and think.

Bill loved poetry and wrote most of his better poetry in his sleep. He would wake with a poem in his head. It never ceased to amaze him how simple writing was when he was in the grove. He created a few on this rock as well. His ears were filled with the sound of thunderous waves crashing all around him. His nostrils were filled with the smell of salt. He started to drift off.

Cold East Point Ferryland

Our Special Place

I am elated, my senses stimulated, the air saturated with the smell of salt.
The cool caress of mist soothes my skin; my soul soars on the northeast wind.
Home to Ferryland! My soul renewed, by the rawness of Nature construed
By a God that makes this place an altar of his saving grace.

This is the place of renewal!
My senses fill with ocean scent. The soothing sound of energy spent,
By thunderous waves, and whistling winds, that rend and tear,
The ragged cliffs to glistening sand, shrouded in the misty air.

My energy rocks waits to couch my form.
The moon's magic illuminates mystically to transform
The dark rocks, sand and waves, into a cool luminescent glow
Of crystal waves that ebb and flow.

My soul escapes into the mist, to rise and soar ore Nature's bliss.
I vanish into the scene and disappear, time suspended in the misty air.
A thousand souls blend into one, as Nature's child I again become.

The spirit of the past and I, ride the wind, the waves and sky.
The past, the future, all are one; no cares, no woes, possessions none.
My God surrounds me everywhere, salt, sand, sea, and air.

I took my daughter Rebecca there, that she and I might forever share,
A Special Place, our souls call home; to join our hearts where ere we roam.
To join our hearts, when joys forgot, we mediate upon this spot.
Our souls will meet were ere we be, in lovely Ferryland by the Sea.

As Bill lay on the rock, seething waters boiled all around him. Deafening waves exploded into crystal rockets releasing their stores of pent up energy in an explosive show of sound and fury. The symphony of sight, sound and smell was punctuated with the haunting cry of sea gulls flying over head, searching the kelp laden shoals for mussels to feed their young. His nostrils filled with ocean scent, a cool mist blanketing his skin. As he focused on the sea gulls flying over head, he was suddenly aware of the scent of a woman. The scent enveloped him filled his lungs and went into every pore in his body. He felt warm. He became aware of the blood cursing through his veins. His heart beat drowned out all other sounds. He had been encompassed by the womb of Mother Nature, warm secure, nurturing. He no longer felt the cold hard rock pressing into his back; instead he was completely blanketed by a warm comforting radiation of pure love. It was if he had returned again to his mother's womb. There, secure, his every need would be taken care of. No worries, no fear, no hunger, his ears filled with the sound of nature's heart, his body heated by undulating rhythms of life's river of blood. He was in heaven. He started to soar and became unaware of time. He felt himself blended into the scene and his natural boundaries of flesh disappeared. He had become transported. As he looked down on the rock on where he had had lain, he could no longer see himself. Everything that had happened in the past was immediately apparent to him. He was able to travel through time as if there was no time. Everything that ever existed was still there. He saw spirits of the past everywhere. One of these spirits arrived like a comet from out of nowhere and possessed him. Suddenly he was able to transport to any planet or galaxy he wished in an instant. There was no time, no space. Distance had no meaning. He found out later that the spirit that had possessed him was an Oracle of the highest magnitude. The Oracle, a seeker, was from the planet Perpetua and was on a journey of discovery. By enveloping Bill the oracle had taken Bill on his journey with him. What the oracle would learn on his timeless journey through the cosmos would be shared with Bill as their cosmic energies were now intermingled. What he would see Bill would see. Bill had become a seeker and was going to Perpetua, the Garden of Eden.

Chapter II

TALES FROM THE LAND WHERE THERE WAS NO TIME

Somewhere in the center of the Multiverse, in one of its billions of Universes there existed a galaxy in which there were sixteen suns that formed a perfect sphere. These sixteen suns were in perfect balance and rotated around a single planet in its center, a place where all things in nature were in perfect harmony. The planet was equidistant from all the sixteen suns making the temperature perfect for sustaining Life. The amount of sunlight and water were perfect for growing things. The sixteen suns were equidistant from each other, and from the planet Perpetua. No sun had more influence on the planet than any of the other sixteen suns. Occasionally a comet or an asteroid from some other galaxy would stray into the sphere of influence of the sixteen suns and disturb that perfect harmony, but only temporarily. The planet was called Perpetua because there was no time. There was no time because the planet being in the center of everything in the Multiverse did not rotate. This gave the planet special properties that did not exist anywhere else in the Multiverse. The planet of Perpetua, being in the center of everything, was held suspended in perfect balance by the sixteen suns. The planet did not move or rotate. There no acceleration or deceleration, and no change in velocity. Light was distributed evenly all around. There was no night, no ocean tides, no wind, no erosion, no volcanoes, and no destruction. Simply put, there was nothing on Perpetua by which to measure time, and hence no need for time. There was no future, no past, only now. It was a virtual Garden of Eden. Perhaps it was the Garden of Eden.

On the planet of Perpetua there existed no plants or animals. Animals eat each other and this causes competition and disrupts harmony. In this land of harmony there was no natural death. Death when it occurred was usually accidental. This does not mean that there was no life in Perpetua, there was lots of life, but life existed in the form of beings that fed on sunlight since sunlight was in abundance and always in the perfect amount. Because there was no wind, no night, no death, the life forms had no need for roots to anchor them. Since the planet was at the very center of the universe and did not rotate on its own axis, or circle any other celestial body, it had special properties. Things happened on Perpetua that did not happen anywhere else in the entire universe. For instance there was no gravity and consequently every life form could levitate at will. Travel could be at any speed they desired and required minimal expenditure of energy. They could exist in any form, shape, color, or consistency they wished. They could blend with the rocks, the water, and the air. These *"Polymorphs"* possessed the ability to take any shape they wanted, to go anywhere they wanted and were constantly on the move except when they gathered to share some thoughts because it was always exciting to share thoughts and learn new things. The Polymorphs called themselves *Seekers* because they were always moving and always looking to learn new things.

This made Perpetua a most beautiful place with its plethora of colors and shapes and smells because the seekers loved variety. On planet earth thousands of galaxies away in another universe, conformity was encouraged and individuality discouraged, and new ideas were frowned upon, but here in Perpetua the Joie *de Vie* was in discovery and knowledge. Here, things did not grow old, here there was no greed, no power, no hunger, no fear, no death no competition. Here there was only knowledge and the search for knowledge. It was Paradise. However, Paradise was about to change. The change would be subtle at first. It would seem innocuous but it was relentless and would eventually bring Paradise to a crashing end.

Originally the thing that motivated the seekers was the search for knowledge since they did not need to look for food or worry about sickness, cold, or death. The search for knowledge and truth pre-occupied and motivated all seekers; some however had more knowledge than others and in this land of perfection this disparity of knowledge was the only imperfection. At first glance this might seem of little importance; however eventually it became the source of such discord that it threatened not only the peace and harmony of the various villages but the very existence of the planet itself.

The seekers though close to perfection were not without faults. The difference in the level of knowledge that existed between various seekers grew over the millennia and eventually led to a difference of power. Some of the more enlightened seekers used their knowledge for the good of all seekers and they were considered oracles and held in high esteem. Other more knowledgeable seekers used their knowledge to acquire more power and were eventually corrupted by the very power they craved. Like other life forms in the Multiverse, such as people here on Earth, the seekers suffered from all the ailments that a difference of power brings. As the power balance shifted, so grew vanity and its ugly sister intolerance. Those who "thought they knew" felt a sense of superiority and treated those who "supposedly knew less" with indifference and intolerance. Sometimes they would use their knowledge to exert power over their less fortunate neighbors. Sometimes they would use their power to accumulate wealth and that wealth spawned greed. These *Power Seekers* would accumulate wealth by any means possible, such as depriving their so called friends of their wealth. The weapon they would always use was knowledge, and knowledge was power. Those that understood this basic principle did everything they could to limit the access to knowledge of their less insightful brother. Soon power and not knowledge became the driving force of a small group of seekers and they set out to control all access to knowledge; by centralizing control of the media, by censorship, by classifying documents in the name of national security. To enhance their influence the Power Seekers restricted access to knowledge. Education then became, not the pursuit of truth, but a weapon to ensure conformity, control and maintenance of the status quo. In fact this new direction of the seekers changed Perpetua from what was a perfect world into a very imperfect world and Paradise was transformed.

Now since the driving force of Perpetua was no longer the pursuit of knowledge but of power, the perfect harmony that had resonated through Perpetua was lost and was replaced by greed, intolerance, oppression and fear. The *Power Seekers*, not having had power before were unaware, that power corrupts and absolute power corrupts absolutely.

The transformation of Perpetua was slow and corrosive. The Power Seekers told the Average Seekers in Perpetua that their system of governance was the best that ever existed. They were told that they had freedom. The Average Seekers failed to see the dangers of centralization of the corporate media, of government secrecy, of secret societies, of classification of documents in the name of national security. The Average Seeker was told that secrecy was necessary for security and that some freedom had to be given up in the name of greater security. What they failed to see was that those who sacrificed freedom for security ended up with neither. The Seekers were given the illusion of freedom since all the choices were predetermined by the centralized, concentrated corporate media which was controlled by a very few of the most powerful Seekers. Free speech was curtailed in the name of patriotism. Dissenters were labeled traitors and prisons were built to house the dissenters. Indoctrination became the norm. Seekers were told what was good and what was evil, for instance, in some parts of Perpetua, not all colors were tolerated and white became right and black became evil. The Power Seekers in an effort to control knowledge restricted travel, and villages became the norm. Like minded people were herded into villages with those who thought similarly to discourage exchange of ideas. Everywhere villagers put up barriers to separate their villages from other villages where seekers thought differently.

Communication between villages was discouraged and different languages were used in different villages to discourage communication and cooperation. It became more difficult to share knowledge. People were taught to fear the unknown. Violence was used to instill fear, and fear was used as a pretext to restrict freedom. Each village was told that they were right and the other villages were wrong. Fear of change, misunderstanding, intolerance and hatred became the currency of the land. Freedom of thought became a crime. Flags were given to the people to identify them and patriotism was seen as more honorable and valuable that the search for knowledge. Words long in existence were given different meanings. Hate became love, lies became truth, conformity became freedom, and evil became good. Misinformation, disinformation, propaganda were used by all media to promote confusion and fear. The corporate media once the champion of civil liberties' were now part of the problem and could no longer be trusted. The small independent news outlet was becoming extinct. Large conglomerates owned by the Power seekers successfully manipulated the masses making the rich richer and the poor poorer. Freedom of choice had been lost.

As the Power seekers became more powerful and more greedy they began to disagree with each other and tried to gain more power at the expense of each other. Each tried to bring more villages under their influence and soon Countries were established. Freedoms were further curtailed; borders, travel restrictions, trade disagreements, and poverty became the norm. With all this dissention, restriction of freedom and knowledge, with all the patriotism, borders and languages, with all the hate and greed; came misunderstanding. Misunderstanding was used to promote wars. Wars were used to further concentrate power in the hands of the Power Seekers. Paradise had been transformed and lost.

Chapter III

THE TRANSFORMATION

As Bill travelled back and forth through time and space with the Oracle the similarities of regression, disintegration and corruption between Perpetua and Earth were striking. The transformation from *Utopia* in Perpetua, and *Eden* on Earth, had resulted in many types of governance within the villages of each country. Interesting enough no matter what the type of governance espoused within each country and village the result was still the same. Everywhere access to knowledge and curtailment of freedom was the blueprint used by the Power Seekers, to maintain and concentrate their control of the masses. Some countries called their governance Democracy, others a Republic, some called it Communism, others a Dictatorship, and still others Socialism, but in reality there was no difference between them all. They all had a hierarchy of rich and poor. In all the societies, in all the countries, the rich got richer and the poor got poorer. Corruption and greed ruled the day. The governments were filled with politicians who never told the truth, the leaders could not get elected without the support of the press which was controlled by the rich and powerful. The few leaders that tried to do the right thing for the masses were usually assassinated or framed by some form of scandal which was disseminated by the media even if it were untrue. Lies became truth, and truth became lies. In countries where there were elections, and supposedly a choice, all candidates were preselected by the powerful elite; votes were bought, truth was censored. Since it took vast wealth to be elected, and since they controlled the media, the rich and powerful always got their way. Since every candidate was owned by the wealthy, it did not matter who won the election, it was always their man. The villagers unaware of this paradigm, were happy since they thought their vote made a difference and everyone danced and sang because they felt so lucky to be free, unlike their neighboring country which wasn't blessed with their system of governance.

Everywhere the Power Seekers were able to dominate and control the villagers. Next they gave the villagers religion and told the villagers that their religion was right and that those who believed in a different religion were wrong. They gave the villagers organized sport so that they would have something to cheer about and would not spend so much time thinking about politics. They created banks and debt and controlled the money supply so that the masses would have to use their currency in trade. Because the Power seekers had absolute control over the money supply they were able to create boom and bust cycles, inflation, taxation and keep the villagers poor. The Power Seekers who were bankers convinced governments to give them the power to print money and with that power they were able to eventually subjugate all governments to do their bidding no matter what the electorate wished.

> *"Give me the power to issue a nation's money;*
> *then I do not care who makes the law."*
> Anselm Rothschild

The Power Seekers created secret societies and organizations and used them to ferment hate and dissension amongst various countries and groups within countries. Religious and political differences were used to promote unrest and war. The Power Seekers (banksters) would create dissention and then would sell weapons to both sides, finance the war on both sides and again finance the reconstruction that inevitably resulted from such wars. By such means they were able to amass vast fortunes and used their money to promote globalization and further concentrate their power and enslave the unsuspecting masses. They would use drugs to addict the masses and destroy their free will. The power seekers hated knowledge and truth, they were masters of deception and had done it so well that the villagers were unaware that they existed in a matrix of false perception. Not cognizant of the paradigm of lies and deception in which they existed the masses were unaware that they had been enslaved.

And finally in the land where there was no time (Perpetua) the concept of time was introduced to further control and enslave the masses. Clocks were invented. Villagers were brainwashed that time was important. That everyone must work so many hours and only allowed a brief time each day for rest and play. Young seekers were sent to school for mind control under the guise of seeking knowledge. Older seeders became slaves in factories, and older less productive seekers were destroyed and recycled, so now death was introduced into the world in the name of efficiency.

In Perpetua and on Earth, not all were complacent and so easily controlled. Some rebelled against their loss of freedoms and particularly against the concept of time and the enslavement that came with it. These were essentially voices in the wilderness, but they did offer insights that kept the dream of freedom alive.

In both planets Perpetua and Earth, those of the oracle class had developed the ability to travel through time and space by assuming the form of pure energy. They could travel the cosmos at will and could observe and compare how things were evolving in both planets.

The Oracle in his travels to earth had determined that things were evolving in a very similar manner on that planet. In fact on Earth things had advanced even further towards total control and enslavement of the populace. The banksters on Earth had successfully moved away from the gold standard and were now able to print money out of thin air. They were able to deflate and inflate economies at will by regulating the money supply. By so doing they could create boom and bust cycles which led to bankruptcies on an unprecedented scale. Deregulation of the banking system by corrupt politicians led to wild speculation by banks with people's money and the rich got richer and the poor got poorer. One percent of the people held ninety percent of the wealth. Debt rose to unprecedented levels and whole countries were going bankrupt. Since money could be printed out of thin air by the banksters, they were able to finance, insurrection, insurgencies, terrorists, standing armies, and destabilize governments and economies. World domination was the objective and soon the world economy was about to collapse.

On Earth people had become enslaved to debt and had lost their governance, as their choices of politicians were all controlled by the power seekers. The politicians in power all had the same message. Those politicians with a different message were not heard as the corporate media filtered the message that was presented to the masses. A few politicians like John F Kennedy, aware of the paradigm, tried to break the hold of the international bankers. Those that tried to change the system were assassinated or eliminated in some way. Others outside of politics such as poets and authors were still able to share their knowledge of the truth as absolute control of the written word had not yet been achieved. The hope still existed that the truth would eventually speak to the masses and that change could still occur. Perhaps these voices in the wilderness would someday be able to obliterate the dark cloud of oppression that was blanketing planet earth. Change if it were to occur on earth would have to come from the bottom up. Perhaps there would be cataclysmic violence. Time would tell.

Bill on his journey with the Oracle, to Perpetua and through time, had witnessed the progression to enslavement. He realized that the situation in the land of Perpetua was very similar to that on earth. Perhaps both planets could learn from each other. There was always hope.

Meanwhile, most people unaware of the *Matrix* in which they existed, remained oblivious to the root cause of their problems and just worked harder and harder, and went faster and faster forgetting the important things in life.

A Dreaded Momentum

With blurring speed and numbing haste
Our lives proceed at record pace
Days so full of work and care
Robots blind and unaware

Each hectic day we rise and run
Compete to get our duties done.
The air a soup of electronic waves
Bombard the mind until it raves.

Like greyhounds, after rabbits run
We have no time for setting sun.
Computers, videos, TV screens
Replace the sane and natural scenes

Trapped in cars, in unending line
We race around, a slave to time.
Like hamsters on the spinning wheel,
No time to stop and think and feel.

Look to the snails! No race to run.
Take our time, enjoy the sun.
For life we live and do not see,
As we race to get from A to B.

Most of the Seekers on Perpetua and people on Earth were unaware that they had lost their freedom; they were unaware that they had lost paradise because the truth was always hidden under the guise of National security. Propaganda had convinced them that their way was the right way and they could not see the truth and were not open to alternate messages that would bring the necessary change. The masses knew one thing and one thing only; they were right and the other guy was wrong. Some however knew the truth, and although very few in number, tried to warn the masses in their writings and their poetry. They would grow in numbers as time would pass. Would the masses see in time before it was too late? Would they believe? Would they understand?

Chapter IV

TYPES OF KNOWLEDGE

The evolution of society on Earth and on Perpetua had taken strikingly similar paths. In all of the many villages in Perpetua and on earth there were seekers of truth and knowledge and like all villages everywhere where seekers live in large numbers there was a hierarchy of power and knowledge. All villages essentially had a hierarchy, which on first inspection might look different but on closer scrutiny were in reality very similar. In all the villages there were seekers who continually sought to increase their power and influence at every opportunity. To maintain that power and influence in all the villages the Power Seekers did essentially the same thing although by slightly different methods. They all sought to control knowledge, and one of the ways you do that was to promote conformity.

There existed essentially four basic types of villagers. There were the villagers that simply "did not know, they were called the *Innocents*. They were like newborn children. They had not yet acquired knowledge and were quite malleable, and like sponges were capable of learning a lot if placed in a learning environment. They were open-minded. They with time usually learned enough to move to another higher class of thinking.

The second type was a very stagnant group. They simply did not know, that they did not know. They knew enough to know that they knew something, but not enough to know that they knew very little. They were a docile group as a rule. They did not ask questions and usually went with the flow and trusted their leaders. They typically exhibited the herd mentality. They were closed minded and incapable of learning, blind to corruption and trusting. They had no desire to change or to search for truth, they were called the *Ignorant*.

The third group "thought they knew enough", but in reality they knew just enough to be dangerous and were resistant to change. They were called the *Deluded*. They formed the ruling class in most villages and were quit intolerant of the other types of villagers. They were slightly aware that there may be gaps in their knowledge base and that there may be better ways of doing things but they feared change. They liked to maintain the status quo and its hierarchy with them at the top. A deluded belief in this concept gave them a false sense of entitlement that drove them to dominate all the other groups. They had very little ability to empathize. They falsely believed that what was good for them should be good for everybody. To them might was right. A lot of religious zealots, politicians, wealthy businessmen, and CEO's fell into this category. They in turn feared most the fourth group "those that knew they do not know", for these were the *Truth Seekers* and the only group powerful enough to see through the matrix of deception.

The last group, the Truth Seekers, *knew just enough to know that they did not know*. This group contained the academics and the scholars. They loved to pursue knowledge and the more they learned the more they realized that they needed to learn. These *Truth Seekers* had as their main driving force the pursuit of knowledge. This last group was actually the wisest.

These *Truth Seekers* had the good of all the citizens at heart for they sought the truth and knew that truth would set them free. This fourth group, the *Truth Seekers*, could be divided into two sub-groups; the "*wise*" because they knew enough to be able ask the right questions. This group contained professors, teachers, philosophers, artists, writers, poets, theologians, theologians, preachers, physicians etc. They also sought truth but they were restricted by brains that thought laterally and were confined to thinking inside the box. The highest functioning subgroup of the *Truth Seekers* was the "*Oracles*" who could think outside of the box and tap into the cosmic consciousness. They knew that there were no answers, there were only questions. Members of the *Oracles Class* on earth and in Perpetua numbered very few, they usually resided in places that were isolated and away from the maddening crowds, places where there was lots of opportunity to meditate, a practice similar to the Buddhist

Monks on earth who lived high in the mountains of Tibet. A few of the more outstanding Oracles would be Jesus, Mohammed, Buddha, and Mahatma Gandhi.

In all the countries and villages of Perpetua and earth the four basic types of villagers existed. Politics and Religion were always hot and divisive topics. In every village and country the group that usually amassed the most power and influence and were most likely to screw things up was the third group the ones that "knew they knew; the *deluded* group that included politicians and religious zealots.

The following sequence of events was witnessed by Bill and the Oracle on their travels and serves to illustrate how things can go wrong even when the intentions are good if minds, even ones that are in search of truth, are not open and are resistant to change.

VILLAGE OF MISUNDERSTANDING

The four tribes of the village often agreed to disagree, but there were many who felt that might was right and they usually, in the more serious matters, had their way and as a result chaos and disharmony usually ruled the day. Rarely on extremely important matters, when there was an impasse, the ruling class would defer to a higher authority and consult the oracle that lived in the mountains, on the island of wisdom, for he was known to be in tune with the cosmic consciousness and for as long as seeker memory existed was never wrong. Sometimes they would heed the advice given, but usually would not since 'They knew they knew'

Dissention was sweeping the land and the four tribes were on the verge of war over the latest important issue. The tribe known as "Innocents" did not know what color God was. Some believed he was white, others grey, and still others believed he had no color at all. They simply did not know. The tribe known as *Ignorant* believed that god was black. The tribe known as the *Deluded* believed that god was a male. And the tribe known as *Wise* believed that God was a female. The debates were hot and heavy; tensions were rising, as the policy meeting of the four tribes was drawing to a close. War clouds were in the air. Finally it was agreed by all that each would consult the oracle and all would abide by the oracles decision.

The *Innocents* went to the oracle and asked him what color God was. The oracle asked them what they believed and some responded that God was white, others grey and yet others no color. The oracle met with each of them individually and told each of them that they were right.

The *Ignorant* went to the oracle, and were affirmed when they told the oracle that they believed that God was black. "Indeed" said the oracle" God is Black".

The *Deluded* were affirmed at their meeting with the oracle that God was indeed a male, and the "Wise" were affirmed at their meeting with the oracle that God was indeed a female.

When the four tribes of the village met again, all were excited that each had been assured of their own concept of truth. When they finally discovered that each other tribe had affirmed a different truth, there were accusations of lying and deception and rage ruled the day. War was about to be declared. However, cooler heads prevailed and it was suggested that all four tribes meet with the oracle simultaneously and hear the truth for themselves. Each was still confident that their side was right because the oracle was never wrong.

So, off they went again to visit the oracle across the sea of confusion, up the Mountain of Pain, across the Lake of Hope to the Island of Wisdom, and finally to the Fountain of Knowledge. There each, had to drink from the Fountain of Knowledge before meeting the oracle and then and only then, if their mind was open, and if their souls were filled with the right amount of humility, would the fountain of knowledge give them the gift of wisdom, so that they would understand the words of the oracle.

They all arrived at the Oracle, confident and prepared to celebrate a great victory. When each group presented its case to the oracle, they were again affirmed by the oracle as before. When all the groups finally got together they realized that nothing had changed. Anger and confusion ruled the day. How could each be right when they believed so differently? Weapons were being drawn and war was a breath away. Then one of the tribesmen cried out to the Oracle "How could this be so?"

How could God be both black and white and be both male and female? Silence fell over the confused and angry crowd and the oracle who was never wrong pronounced to the assembly. **"It is so, because you believe it to be so!"**

The seekers of the four tribes did not understand the message. It was too abstract for them. They wanted something simple, something factual, something concrete. They knew the Oracle was always right, but their anger, hatred, greed, self righteousness, and fear of change blinded their eyes and hardened their hearts and as they made their way back to their villages where they continued to argue and be intolerant, each convinced that they were right and the other was wrong.

After the disastrous meeting with the Oracle, back in their villages, life went back to usual. The villagers led by the *Deluded* continued to listen to their favorite propaganda stations, preaching intolerance, hatred, and self righteousness. They continued to spout their patriotic mantras, wave their flags convinced that their way was the right way and that the others were at the worst dangerous and at the best misguided. The seekers as all citizens of Perpetua were called, continued to slave in the factories producing weapons, to protect themselves from those who thought differently, making the Power Seekers rich and keeping them poor. The irony of it all was that nobody was happy not even the rich Power Seekers, who never satiated always, lusted for more.

Chapter V

PARADISE LOST

The various villages of Perpetua and Earth had their share of little daily problems as well and major events. Events like the meeting of the four tribes with the oracle were rare events and soon passed into the subconscious mind of the seekers supplanted by more mundane thoughts of routine which filled their day. Things went on as usual in the villages. The average citizen in both planets were busy, working long hours at jobs producing weapons, paying taxes, and trying to get money to buy things they didn't need. As a result they were too busy to think of a better way. There was no time to meditate. No time to play? No time for family? More time was spent listening to the propaganda machines? Every citizen was told by the Power Seekers that he had to have possessions and more possessions; things like electronic games, TV's, better things than the other seekers. "You won't be happy unless you have this, or unless you have that! You can't afford to take care of your neighbor, but you can afford things, things and more things. Most importantly, you must have weapons, better weapons than the other guy". Newer, better, more! Always newer, better more, until they were poor, all in the name of national security. Instead of becoming strong through mutual love, nurturing, caring and sharing the citizens became greedy, and selfish and fearful that someone, anyone, even their neighbor would take their things away; things that they were told by the propagandists and the Power seekers they needed.

Everyone had forgotten that long ago seekers did quite well without things; seekers shared, cared for each other, protected, each other, shared knowledge, sought truth and were happy. Paradise had been lost. The way to salvation was obvious to the Oracles but not to the average seeker. For the seekers, the loss of love for your fellow being, the loss of humility, the curse of self-righteousness had shut off the fountain of knowledge and prevented them from getting the gift of wisdom and understanding. And the irony of it all was; that the quest for things they did not need, the quest for weapons to keep them safe, the barriers to keep out new and strange ideas, had not made them stronger but had made them fearful, weak and vulnerable, and even more determined to protect their unique way which after all was the best way.

Chapter VI

"BULLYING AND TRANSFORMATION"

Consequences *"I shot an arrow into the air, it fell to earth, I knew not where".* Henry Wadsworth Longfellow

The Oracle and Bill were having an amazing cosmic journey. Bill was learning much as they transported through time and space visiting earth and Perpetua. They decided to investigate a young girl on earth who was standing on the edge of a precipice. The young girl stood teetering on the edge of a cliff, below her lay beautiful fields of flowers. The air was filled with sweet scents and the blue sky was lit by streams of sunlight from the brilliant sun that filled the sky. The peaceful serene scene stood in stark contrast to the panic seething in her chest as the voice within her screamed: "I wish you were dead. I hate you". The voice was her own. After all she was ugly or so they said. She was stupid and worse yet, she wasn't white. At school that day, they had said she was a freak. All the other students in her class were the same, she was different and so they hated her. For months she had been abused, called names, spit on, tripped, pushed, and punched. When she walked bye she could see the other students snickering, whispering, and laughing at her. Some would turn their backs as she approached. Some would change the topic of their conversation, or would stop talking altogether. Some would walk away; some in her presence would invite her classmates to a party deliberately leaving her out. Others, the worst, would totally ignore her and pretend that she just wasn't even there. They were the worst because to them she didn't even exist. She was nothing. She was filled with hate; hate for them and worse hate for herself. She did not deserve to live, she was wasting air.

She could not see a way out. She was trapped, trapped in her ugly body with her stupid mind.

She had tried fighting back, but that made them laugh more. She had run away in tears, but that made them sneer with joy. She had tried cutting her wrists, burning her skin hoping that the physical pain would ease her far greater mental pain, but that only gave her temporary relief, leaving her filled with guilt and shame; shame, not for having done it, but shame because she did not have the courage to go all the way. Shame and disgust because deep down she realized she wanted to be liked by them, and to be one of them, and she hated them and hated herself even more because her desires were a sign of weakness. She looked down into the abyss. A wave of disgust flooded over her otherwise dead body and she threw up so violently that she slipped and fell over the ledge. With a last desperate grasp for life, she grabbed a small plant that had attached itself to the edge of the cliff. Miraculously it held. She hung there perilously for what seemed like an eternity. She did not want to die! She could not climb up; her grip on life was slipping, slipping. Help! Help! She cried, but no one was there to hear. Exhaustion and extreme panic set in. She let go. A thousand feet below the jagged rocks were waiting to devour her. She fainted.

Just as she was about to crash into the rocks below, she found herself flying through space at incredible speed. Her body had become energized, her mind released from its imprisonment of pain. She was back on the ledge as if she hadn't fallen. She had been possessed by the spirit of an oracle who had witnessed her peril. The Oracle being had enlightened her and freed her of the burdens of ignorance, intolerance, and all the evils that had poisoned her soul and destroyed her spirit. She was able to tap into the cosmic consciousness. Briefly she was one with the cosmos and the godlike knowledge that lies therein. Travelling at the speed of thought there were no limits to her imagination. She was able to do incredible things. She was able to see into the future as well as the past. She was able to read minds and more importantly hearts and most important of all was able to find truth. Armed with weapons of discipline, love and the powers of meditation she was able to transport herself instantly all over the entire Multiverse by becoming one with the cosmic consciousness. She had become all knowing and all aware instantly.

An eternity had passed in a few seconds. She had seen the pain of others; she had been able to look into the soul of her tormentors, each and every one of them. In an instant she had been infused with understanding and love not only for herself but for the others, all the others, all who knew pain and suffering. She felt beautiful. She realized that before you can love others you must love yourself. For each and every one of us is beautiful. She knew that those who hated others like she once did really hated themselves. She understood that when she let her tormentors control her feelings, she was giving them power over her. She knew that if she showed them love no matter what they had done, she would have power over them and with that power she could, through love, teach them to love themselves; then and only then could they become capable of loving others. She knew that love is all there is, love is all you need, love would give her power, to heal, to forgive, to become tolerant. Love would make her invincible.

Becoming

Deep inside she lay, hidden by shadows
Unaware of her beauty, unappreciated, unknowing,
She lay there cocooned by walls that closed
around her, shutting out her light.

Seen as an irritant, layers of hurt were heaped upon her,
to keep her in her place. Uncomplaining she laid there,
Her own walls silently growing with time.

Still her beauty was not seen, nor was she appreciated, until one day
The deep seas of oppression that blanketed her were lifted,
And she was washed on unfamiliar shores.

Slowly the light crept into her world,
revealing the beauty that radiated from deep inside her.
And finally, she realized that she had become a thing of great beauty.

She . . . . had become . . . . a . . . PEARL

Becoming Transformed

Beccy's Eyes

There is no crystal starry sky;
No brilliant sunset ore ocean shore;
No infinite view from mountain high;
No clear blue sky ore flowered floor;
No scent so fair; no beauty found;
No nectar sweet this wide world round;
That can compare to the joy I feel . . . .
When I look into . . . .
Beccy's Eyes!

My Beccy's Eyes

Chapter VII

"A COSMIC JOURNEY"

The Oracle had been deep in concentration when a shockwave of discordance penetrated his consciousness. It was so strong that it briefly disrupted the whole harmony of Perpetua. The Oracle shifted his focus, a passenger jet had hit a building on Earth, and thousands were dead. In time millions would die because of it. He transported to Earth. As he approached Earth, a tsunami of pain engulfed him. Although its epicenter was the destroyed building, the wave of pain spread through the universe. The cosmic consciousness had been breached. Now it remained to be seen it the breech would foster a search for truth or a further retreat into self-righteousness and intolerance by all those involved. The butterfly effect would be huge and would last for years.

The Oracle was keenly aware of the parallels between his home of Perpetua and the predicament of planet Earth; the planet was dying. The people of the planet had stopped searching for knowledge and truth; instead greed and intolerance ruled the day. The same forces that were destroying his planet were destroying planet Earth. Unfortunately planet Earth was much further along the path to destruction than his own planet. People there had become addicted to things. Everywhere people had left their tiny villages and had moved to bigger and bigger cities. The automobile had become the dominant force in nature. Everywhere people had stopped talking to people, families no longer sat down and ate together, and instead electronics became the food for their soul. Lacking meaning in their lives people had become addicts; addicted to power, addicted to things, addicted to drugs, addicted to sex. *Everywhere people were looking outside for answers, instead of inward.* People had distanced themselves from nature. No one understood it. People saw themselves as "godlike", as special, above nature and not part of it. Nature could be used and abused as they saw fit. They did not even consider that when they abused nature they abused themselves. They had lost touch with the cosmic consciousness and the chickens were coming home to roost. The forces of greed and power had reshaped the planet, and everything was changing, changing for the worse. There was global warming. Everywhere, thousands of species of plants and animals were disappearing, becoming extinct. Ecosystems were collapsing, and the balance necessary to sustain life and happiness as mankind once knew it, was being disrupted.

Newspapers all over the world were reporting one environmental disaster after another. Perhaps the greatest environmental collapse in human history was that of the northern cod stocks of Newfoundland. After sustaining most of North America and all of Europe for over five Hundred years the cod fishery collapsed due to mismanagement and greed. Over 30,000 Newfoundlanders lost their job and hundreds of villages disappeared. Scientists reported that if fishing around the world were to continue at the same pace, global collapse of all the major marine ecosystems would occur within fifty years. Something had to be done; on a massive scale and it had to be done soon or it would be too late.

No one wanted to give up their things, no one wanted to give up their little bit of power, everyone expected the other guy to do it, and as a result the planet was dying and the future was bleak. People were lying, cheating and stealing to outdo their fellow man, and in the process became the architect of their own undoing. Planet Earth as man***kind*** knew it was dying, and in the cosmic court man would be accused of ***rape*** and ***murder***.

Fish on William Morry's Stage 1960

William Mory the father of the author (standing above), exported light-salted cod to the USA, Carribean, and Europe for almost forty years. He was the last producer / exporter of salt cod in NFLD. His retirement in the late 1980's marked the end of a 500 year era of exporting salt cod. He served on the Nfld Salt Fish Corporation and The Fisheries Council of Canada for many years. In July of 1992 the Nfld Government declared a Moritorium on the cod fishery due to the total collapse of the cod stocks because of overfishing. The cod stocks have never recovered.

The Moratorium

Unused boats, dying in the sun,
Aborted, lifeless, No work is done.
Unseasoned seams, admit the light
Unwetted now, no longer tight.

Harbours void of fishing boats
Oceans free of nets and floats.
Young men gather in early dawn
And sadly talk of days now gone.

Sea gulls dipping in empty seas
Mothers cannot young mouths feed.
Lightened sand in June no more
Since Capelin do not come to shore

Fence posts free of their yoke of nets,
Since now there are no births to set.
All is now in disrepair,
Since there is no need for fishing gear.

Empty sheds and wharves half done,
Untethered anchors in the sun.
Houses empty, with broken panes
Roofs admit the season's rains.

Boats are empty, cars are full
As precious things they push and pull.
As people leave this place called home.
Now greener pastures seek to roam.

The cod are gone! A culture too!
The common thread that saw us through
Five hundred years of strain and toil
The ocean now like dessert soil.

And still they fish, these foreign fleets.
Moved by greed, Great stocks deplete.
Catch them all before you do
Extinction! NO! It can't be true.

Canada Young, Not man, still boy
Must all diplomatic routes employ?
Afraid to take an uncharted way
To protect the stocks from those who prey.

While governments vacillate and sway
Our heritage, it slips away.
Inaction now for far too long.
Too late! The codfish now are gone!

Seagull on rotten boat

Where Did Our Village Go?

Where did our village go? Where did it go?
I hear silence where its spirit used to flow.

No life now on the beaches or the wharves.
No boats to disappear in wild sea troughs

The silence of the dawn like thunder roars,
Since no skiffs depart the wharves to fish the shores.

No laughter where the children used to play,
Now only dreams of scenes of yesterday.

No boys in cut-off boots cutting tongues,
No fence posts where damaged nets were hung.

No beaches lined with miles of drying cod.
No dedicating sealing fleets to God.

No silver sands lightened with capelin spawn.
Nothing now, but silence at break of dawn.

No gulls trailing trap skiffs with their haul.
No Sunday games where men & boys play ball.

No hockey on the pond where we would play.
Since all the youth have left and gone away.

No beaches filled with boats up for repair.
No anchors, nets, and floats a hanging there.

Now all the wharves have sunk in disrepair.
And the shells of boats lie idle rotting there.

The spirit of the past a ghostly thread.
That tells us that our culture's nearly dead.

And I wonder if we can reverse the trend,
Before our village will forever end?

Desert Seas

From my window I see the ocean clear, crystal waters devoid of life
Floats & buoys & nets were there, when men did fish for all their life.
In the silence of the dawn is heard, the lonely cry of the starving bird
Ghostly voices in the shadows say that all must starve or go away.

Silent cries of a village dead, echo in the fishing shed.
Silent boats, silent men, Silenced! Never heard again.
Empty waves wash the sandy shore, where
mating capelin are found no more.

Starving gulls dip in empty seas, crying chicks their mouths can't feed.
In Cabot's day the waters boiled, with breeching back's of cod so plenty.
Now dragging nets are seldom soiled, with
fishes trapped, their meshes empty.

The ocean's floor a desert waste, ploughed to dust by dragger's gates.
No reeds, no kelp, no urchins grow. Over barren soil, dead waters flow.
And still they fish, fuelled by greed. Destroying fish filled with seed.
Destroy their food; destroy their home, until no fish are left to roam.

Uncaring people do not heed, the lessons from past species lost
Powers lust to satisfy, over fish at any cost.
Squid, capelin, herring, cod, destroyed by man, not by God,
By greedy men, who do not care who fish until they disappear?

Worldwide, men rape earth's resource, and
leave us all with but one recourse,
To believe that men will carry on,
Until the entire planet's gone.

Man as God

Mother Nature bruised and battered,
Abused by man, food chains shattered,
Life sustaining womb invaded.
Rapacious man has nature jaded.

Five billion years of life evolving.
Now ending fast, food chains dissolving.
Fertile earth to desert soil,
Pristine pure by pollutants spoil.

Redundant food chains intertwined
Wondrous web by supreme design.
Unraveling fast this wondrous weave.
Destroyed by mans unending greed.

User man inflates his worth
Denies that this is spaceship earth
Thinks that all is here for him
To use destroy at his wish or whim

Man in mirror, God's image sees
And therein lies the fallacy
Has man himself a God become
By Religious faith the damage done.

For once we see ourselves above
We rend ourselves of nature's love
Destroy the living things we see.
And Rape with cold impunity

Extinction is our final end
Unless our wasteful ways we mend
From lofty perch we must return
From natures plan a lesson learn

That man is but a grain of sand
And not the center of God's great plan
And wondrous though all creatures be
God loves them all **equally.**

Everywhere the Oracle could see that man had forgotten core values, and had lost his spiritual connection with nature, everyone was unhappy. Hedonism became the norm, and beauty became only skin deep, and in no one was looking inside for answers, most were looking for love in all the wrong places. Drugs, gambling, sex became the new Gods.

"Ode to the Pitcher Plant"

Quietly she sets her trap,
With nectar sweet and slippery slope
Victim's unsuspecting sap
The deadly nectar with senses doped
Judgement gone, with pleasures feed,
Your soul consumed with lust and greed

Towards the edge you wander near
In pleasure there's no sense of fear
Numbed by nectars sweet appeal
Caution gone, no danger feel
Towards the edge you slowly slide
Seeking treasures deep inside

With sinful ease at her behest
You seek the pleasures of the flesh
Deeper, deeper inside you're drawn
The velvet WALLS become your song
And soon you slide into the well,
That then becomes a living hell

Too late, too late, you realize,
The danger was so well disguised,
For pleasure has a double edge,
And pleasure's path a narrow ledge
The pitcher plant can teach us well,
The path that's sure to lead to Hell.

Pitcher Plant

Dissatisfaction, lies, and deceit spawned a plague of corruption. No longer seeking truth, most people ignored it, a few understood it; of those few, some embraced it, and some tried to escape from it through drugs. Unhappiness and pain were everywhere. People were abused, were abusing; people were ashamed of what they had become.

Hiding my eyes

I couldn't look into his eyes, afraid that he might see;
the person hiding there inside, the person that was me.
The well of hell and shame inside, the failure that I've been.
This shell you see, not really me, my mask for life's routine.

Chorus

For deep inside, a wounded heart, afraid again to soar,
Lies broken battered, shattered, discarded on the floor.
Back then I dreamed the world it seemed a magic place to be.
But life with you changed all of that, changed all that I could be

You stole my dreams. Ripped up my seams, with your cruel reality.
Got in my head, and made me dread everything that's me
You broke me down, trashed my soul, ripped me all to shreds,
and left me lying everywhere, I wished that I were dead.

Chorus

I hide away, and dread the day, the shadows cover me.
The broken Pains that are my eyes, I want no one to see
And now I hide behind these eyes, the Window to my soul.
I look away until the day, when again I will be whole.

Chorus

I can't let them see the mess that is me.
I can't put my heart on display.
Afraid to be seen, Afraid I might see,
So I'll keep hiding my eyes

To escape the pain of reality, people turned to drugs for escape but became even more trapped in a reality of pain.

Take Me in Your Arms {Miss Heroin}

So now, little man, you've grown tired of grass
LSD, goofballs, cocaine and hash,
and someone, pretending to be a friend,
said, "I'll introduce you to Miss Heroin."
Well honey, before you start fooling with me,
just let me inform you of how it will be.

For I will seduce you and make you my slave,
I've sent men much stronger than you to their grave.
You think you could never become a disgrace,
and end up addicted to Poppy seed waste.

So you'll start inhaling me one afternoon,
you'll take me into your arms very soon.
And once I've entered deep down in your veins,
the craving will nearly drive you insane.

You'll swindle your mother and just for a buck.
You'll turn into something vile and corrupt.
You'll mug and you'll steal for my narcotic charm,
only feel contentment when I'm in your arms.

The day, when you realize the monster you've grown,
you'll solemnly swear to leave me alone.
If you think you've got that mystical knack,
then sweetie, just try getting me off your back.

The vomit, the cramps, your gut tied in knots.
The jangling nerves screaming for just one more shot.
The hot chills, cold sweats, and withdrawal pains,
can only be saved by my little white grains.

There's no other way, and there's no need to look,
for deep down inside you know you are hooked.
You'll desperately run to the pushers and then,
you'll welcome me back to your arms once again.

And you will return just as I have foretold!
I know that you'll give me your body and soul.
You'll give up your morals, your conscience, your heart.
And you will be mine until, "Death Do Us Part"
Anonymous

What Lies behind us and what Lies before us are Tiny Matters Compared to What Lies within Us. **Oliver Wendell Holmes**

Despite the obvious warning signs, the Power Seekers still wanted more power. Man had turned away from his quest for knowledge and truth. Greed had led to intolerance, and intolerance had led to war. Everywhere man was killing he fellow man, and the price was death of the soul.

Chapter VIII

"THE PRICE OF KILLING"

The nurse drew up a sedative and approached the young soldier in his bed at the military hospital. He had been screaming in his sleep. His young face scarred by the loss of innocence. His eyes, wild with fear and unimaginable pain, were windows to a soul that had lost its way. His lips trembled; he tried to utter words he could not speak. He was a soldier coming back from the war. The wounds he carried were not those of lost limbs, but the loss of his soul. Unfortunately for him, the war he fought, had followed him home and was now being waged on a new battlefield; one that only he could see. The weapons he needed to win it were different weapons; he had none and did not know where to find them. Hate had been a useful weapon over there, it had served him well, but now the fire of hate was self hate and it terrified him. Once an idealist, he had believed in his country. Now he felt his country's cause unjust. He felt lied to, betrayed. He was ashamed of what his country made him become. He felt alone, isolated and no longer knew who he was. He had no future and was chained to a past that he could not forget. He wanted to run away, but he had nowhere to run too, since he could not run from himself. He had killed others; some of them were younger than his baby brother. Every time he saw his baby brother it reminded him of what he had done. He wanted to kill himself. He could not. He was too much of a coward. He did not belong here. He did not belong anywhere.

The nurse bared his arm, and gave him his sedative. She held his head in her arms and sang him a lullaby. Tears welled up in his eyes and his body convulsed with unspeakable demons trapped inside. He sobbed uncontrollably. She rocked him like a baby as she sang. Eventually he slept.

Aftermath

Deep, dark, deafening, shadows of emptiness fill my soul.

A Black Hole of negativity sucks out all vestiges of life'.

I am the walking dead.

Hemorrhaging hurt rages against the light.

A leadened blanket of despair wraps me, smothers me,

And thickens the air I breathe turning it into a soup

Of pain that drowns my tortured soul.

Endless pervasive pain scours every fiber of my being.

There is no rest, no respite, from the tormenting barbs of regret,

For mistakes I've made, love I've lost, dreams I've dashed

And guilt

Guilt for what I have become, forever mindful

That, the gift of innocence which I have thrown
into the bottomless pit of despair,

Can never again be mine.

Choices

How does one forgive oneself, when others will not forgive?

How does one leave the past behind, when the stain of shame

Is the light that guides your way?

How does one see beauty through eyes that burn with pain?

How does one look out, when the walls you build are high?

How does one move forward, when you know not where you are?

How does one escape, when you're afraid to dream?

How does one love others, when you cannot love yourself?

When rejection, indifference, and distain are all you know,

Why would you want to try?

What Choice have you got?

None!

Therefore you must!

ME . . . . . Alone

Where do I Belong? Alone? or with them!
Where do my feelings take me . . . . when I am alone?
Towards tranquility and contentment or . . . . towards
My Destruction! . . . 'The pleasures of the Lonely
Path' . . . Not the pleasures of sharing!

I know that I don't want to be there . . . . Alone!
Yet I find things there, that I can't find . . . . with them.
The pleasures attract me . . . No, no possess me, and they scare me.
That's why . . . . I don't like to go there . . . . alone.

I'd rather be here . . . . With Them,
then be here . . . . . alone . . . . with me.
I like the me, they make me become . . . . with them,
Unlike the me . . . . I am Alone.

Is it the 'me' I don't like or 'me alone'? Or is it the me I become when I am
. . . . Alone!

Conversation Between Us

I wish I could tell her what I did!

She wouldn't understand, ... she's not you.

You see she knows me, better than you do, ... 'the bad side'.

It scares her, and it should scare me too . . . it does . . . but not enough

. . . . to make me stop . . . . !

That's why, ... she must never know.

The Sparrow's Heart

I shot a sparrow as a boy, to see if I could do it.
It did not move! It did not fly! The missile went right through it.

It did not fall from its lofty stance. I killed it instantly;
Snuffed out its life, without a chance, for all eternity.

The pellet pierced its tiny heart, and with it mine as well;
For I did regret the deadly dart, as my eyes with tears did swell.

This gentle bird was killed by me. Was killed because I could.
For an ugly battle raged in me, between the evil and the good.

The evil deeds that we do, insure that we not fly.
Like the little bird, I never flew. I had no heart to try.

Lessons from a Field Mouse

A little field mouse came up to me, while I was mowing hay.
I grabbed a stick that was nearby, and swept the mouse away.

Cute mouse he was, a standing there, not meaning any harm.
He looked at me and I at he, the moment seemed so long.

In youth I did a cruel thing, I regret until this day.
The stick I gave a mighty swing and swept the mouse away.

Why did I do it? He hurt no one! In fact I was entranced,
By the little creature of the field, that I had met by chance.

Man's disrespect exists within us all.
We all must come to understand, the gifts of creatures small.

For we must learn to treasure, all creatures of this earth,
They fill our lives with pleasure, from the moment of our birth.

So little mouse forgive me, for you have taught me well,
Respect's the way to heaven. Disrespect's the way to hell.

Chapter IX

"LOVE HURTS"
SONGS AND POEMS

As the Oracle travelled around planet Earth, he looked into people's hearts everywhere, and everywhere he looked he saw pain. The pursuit of things, better things, and more things had replaced the search for truth and knowledge. Everywhere people were hurting, relationships were damaged. Some had started out in love but for various reasons, without wanting to, had driven their love away. Hearts had lost their way. Hearts were abused. Hearts were broken. Hurting hearts once in love were afraid to love again. Some were so focused on careers and getting ahead that they simply lost their way. Some did not recognize it when they had it. Everyone wanted love and most did not know where to find it. The world was a mess. People were hurting.

Cocooned

Cocooned inside, your feelings hide, your beauty locked away.
Your heart in doubt, afraid to shout, in control you have to stay.
Your wounded heart has split apart, afraid again to soar.
The safest way, you have to stay, inside the bolted door.

You yearn to seek the treasures deep, inside a love that's true.
Yet you afraid to weave the braid, and do as lovers do.
You're holding back, afraid to crack, your walls so wide and high.
Why can't you free your love for me, like wings that ride the sky?

Each time you see, you withdraw from me, cocooned inside your shell,
Push me away. Those words won't say. Make life a living hell.
You wound my heart tear me apart. To go or shall I stay?
Don't make my fire, a funeral pyre. Don't drive my love away.

Just take a chance on this romance; you'll never rue the day
I'll dry your tears, take all your fears, and blow them all away
You're in my heart, till death us part, I'll never go astray
I promise you, my love is true. Forever and a day.
I promise you, my love is true. Forever and a day

Can be sung to the music of Cold Cold Heart

I'm Living a Lie

This poem is a song and can be sung to the tune of "Your Cheating Heart" by Hank Williams

I'm living a lie, our love it has died.
I don't want you with me, not by my side.

Your touch is so cold, my heart is like stone.
You torture me so, I wish you would go, and leave me alone.

I'm living a lie, when I look in your eyes.
I long for the days, when my soul was alive.

You never say darling I love you so.
The loss of the flame, we're not the same. It tortures me so.

I'm living a lie wanting your heart
I sense we are slowly drifting apart.

But you never tell me what I want to hear
You never touch; you never say "I love you dear".

I'm living a lie, I wish it not so
I wish for the nights of not long ago.

When I'd look in your eyes and you'd look in mine.
Our love song would play, till break of day, our bodies entwined.

I wonder what happened. I wish it not so.
I wish you would tell me that you love me so.

I can't live without you, I can't live at all.
I'm longing to hear, that you love me dear. It frightens me so.

So what do I do now, without you I'm gone.
And with you I'm dying. I've hungered so long.

I'll pretend that you love me, like it used to be.
It must not end, I must pretend, and Live a Lie.

The Ember of my heart

Each day with leaden feet I go to work,
And wear a plastic smile to hide my pain.
I hide behind my eyes that won't engage,
And wish I was a baby once again.

I have no arms to bundle all my shreds,
No caring arms to gather all my tears.
No tender arms to blanket me with love,
No gentle arms to dissipate my fears.

My broken heart is there for all to see.
I try to hide it deep inside of me.
Smoldered by the blanket of my pain,
I wonder if my heart will flame again.

The blood pumped through my veins is icy cold.
The heart once young with love has now grown old
No longer can my shattered spirit soar,
Trapped by the ash of love that is no more.

The covered mirror cannot hide my past.
The walls I built are made of broken glass.
My silent screams are there for all to hear,
And still I cannot find someone to care.

When I come home from work at end of day,
I drink the wine to wash my pain away.
The empty bottle does not fill my soul.
I need somebody's love to make me whole

A friend looked into my heart the other day.
The ashes of my pain, he blew away.
The ember of my love was lying there,
His gentle leaves of hope replaced despair

I no longer look into the broken glass,
That covers all the pain that was my past.
The world outside will never look the same.
The ember of my heart is now a flame.

Morning Thoughts

Sometimes at night while you rest
I rise up from my place,
With loving wonder in my breast
And gaze upon your face.

If you were only in my eyes,
When I'm staring there at you
You would know and realize,
That I love and honour you.

You lie there soft and quiet,
Oblivious to my stare.
Not knowing how great the love
That lies beside you there.

Yet when you wake I cannot find.
The words that can impress
The burning passion that you'll find
Deep within my breast.

You will not let me in your heart.
Your ears they do not hear.
Your WALLS protect you from my love
And fill my soul with fear

That someday we will drift apart
The wounds will be too great
Those WALLS, so high, will break my heart
And crush it with its weight.

Love her all the way

Pj Morry March 11, 2012

If the one you love, is building walls so high,
Around a bleeding heart, that's so afraid to try,
When time is long, every minute might seem, just like a day.
When words don't work, no matter what you say.

If the tears you shed are drowning out your flame;
And your skies above are always filled with rain;
Please don't give up, someday I know she will love again.
The driest skies with time will hold some rain.

The winds of change will blow your pain
away. Your skies of grey will be blue again someday.
Please don't give up. Give her all your love, what else can you do?
Someday you'll see her light come shining through.

Give her all your love; she will learn to fly,
Far above her wall of tears that seem so high.
Each day you'll see, her love will grow, in each and every way.
You can't go wrong, if you love her all the way.
Just go ahead and love her all the way.

Sung to the air of "Cry" by Crystal Gayle

Journey to the Ice Fields

The love boat brings love to the glacier, or does the glacier bring ice to the love boat?

For some the relationship will be cemented, enhanced, renewed, touched by the majesty of nature, with feelings tingling and dancing like rain on the water, senses all alive smell touch, hearing, sight. Pounding rhythms of adrenalin permeate solitude of ethereal bliss.

For others, the chill of the ice fields will blanket them and turn their chilled near dead hearts to stone, as they realize that the magic outside cannot be found again inside.

For yet others, the meeting of the two worlds will stoke the fires of confusion, convulsing their souls, creating an atmosphere of volatility.

Which one am I on this journey? The journey is not yet over, but the ice is near Very Near!

Chapter X

WHAT OF SEXUALITY?

On his journey around planet earth the Oracle, with his passenger Bill had observed that the earth was rich in diversity of life; from plants to animals, from bacteria to elephants, and within the human race itself, variety and diversity were the dominant themes. Although there were tremendous differences in the physical form and function of every living thing, there was also incredible variety in social structures, and within the social structure itself, the gender of a being seemed to be its primary defining characteristic. Gender dictated a being's role within the community; in fact, it seemed to be the key element in determining a being's future, socially, biologically, philosophically, economically, and politically! Confronted with the awareness of how significant one's gender was, the Oracle couldn't help but begin to ruminate on the purpose of sexuality itself.

Some social structures were matriarchal, others patriarchal. Some ruled by consensus, others by a single dominant male or female. Species such as the Bonono Monkey solved all their disputes through copulation, others like man through mutilation. In the ants everything was organized to protect the queen and her phenomenal reproductive capability. Some societies only protected their young for a few months after birth, others for years and others not at all. Some animals and plants reproduced asexually, like amoebas where they just simply divided themselves in two. Others sought a mating partner. Some animals had both male and female sex organ in one body. In some animals the males would carry and birth the young, in others it was the female who gave birth. Every society had mating rules and rituals. In some species such as lions it was the biggest, strongest, meanest males, which got to fertilize the female.

In other species like the peacock it was the prettiest males that got the job done. In songbirds the bird with the prettiest song got to do the honors. Some species were asexual; they simply reproduced by dividing themselves! Other species sought a mating partner, some species chose same sex partners, some chose multiple partners, some mated for life with a single partner. In all of nature sexuality was varied. There was no one size fit all construct.

What then the Oracle wondered was the purpose of sexuality? Did it exist purely to allow for the reproduction of living things; or was there more to it than that?

The Oracle thought long and hard about that question. He thought about all the sexual variety he had observed in nature. He'd seen that in mankind that variety, which is so common in nature, had bred intolerance. He had seen gay rights parades, and then had seen violence and hatred exhibited towards gay people from other humans across the globe. He had seen sexual repression. He had seen organized religions speaking of love one minute and showing intolerance the next. Everywhere there was violence and hatred displayed towards homosexuals. He did not understand this because there was no similar display of violence towards homosexuals in the animal kingdom even though homosexuality existed. Why was it so different with humans? Why the intolerance? Perplexed by the contentious nature which surrounded all things sexual in human societies the Oracle decided to focus on the basics of sexual behavior in search for an explanation as to why things were vastly different in human societies as opposed to animal societies. To the Oracle the answer to the question, "What is the purpose of sexuality, would be found in looking at the animal kingdom, particularly species that were evolutionary older than man. The Oracle was not surprised to find that the human species of animal on the planet were by far the most diverse in their sexual behaviors. He was however unprepared for the emotional, spiritual, and moral attachment that humans brought to the act of sex.

In his readings the Oracle came across a scientist named Bagemihl whose life work has been the study of sexual behavior in the animal kingdom. According to Bagemihl; "the animal kingdom [does] it with much greater sexual diversity—including homosexual, bisexual and non-reproductive sex—than the scientific community and society at large have previously been willing to accept." [1, 2] Current research indicated that various forms of **Same Sex Behavior** are found throughout the animal kingdom. [5] A new review made in 2009 of existing research showed that same-sex behavior is a nearly universal phenomenon in the animal kingdom, common across species applying the term *homosexuality* to all sexual behavior (copulation, genital stimulation, mating games and sexual display behavior) between animals of the same sex. In most instances, it is presumed that the homosexual behavior is but part of the animal's overall sexual behavioral repertoire, making the animal "bisexual" rather than "homosexual" as the terms are commonly understood in humans,[16] but cases of homosexual preference and exclusive homosexual pairs are known." Bagemihl again observes "Some species masturbate, have oral sex, and use sex toys.""Some species are predominantly homosexual, most are bisexual, and most combine sex for pleasure with sex for procreation. Some animals form long term pair-bonds (sometimes lifelong). Some animals rear their young in same sex pair bonds. Bagemihl estimates that same sex relationships probably occur in 15-30% of the 1 million species of animals that are known to exist.

The Oracle referenced other research he explored on sexuality in the animal kingdom; "One fundamental premise in social debates has been that homosexuality is unnatural. This premise is wrong. Homosexuality is both common and highly essential in the lives of a number of species," explains Peter Boeckman, who is the academic advisor for the "Against Nature's Order?" exhibition.

The most well-known homosexual animal is the dwarf chimpanzee; one of humanity's closest relatives. The entire species is bisexual. Sex plays a conspicuous role in all their activities and takes the focus away from violence, which is the most typical method of solving conflicts among primates and many other animals. "Sex among dwarf chimpanzees is in fact the business of the whole family, and the cute little ones often lend a helping hand when they engage in oral sex with each other." Lions are also homosexual. Male lions often band together with their brothers to lead the pride. To ensure loyalty, they strengthen the bonds by often having sex with each other. Homosexuality is a social phenomenon and is most widespread among animals with a complex herd life.

Homosexual behavior has been observed in 1,500 animal species, the range is vast and varied and includes dolphins, whales, monkeys, geese, lions, crabs, and invertebrates such as worms. Animals that live a completely homosexual life can also be found. This occurs especially among birds that will pair with one partner for life, which is the case with geese and ducks. Four to five percent of the couples are homosexual. Single females will lay eggs in a homosexual pair's nest. It has been observed that the homosexual couples are often better at raising the young than heterosexual couples. All these observations beg the question: If a female has sex with a male one time, for the purpose of reproduction, but thousands of times with another female, is she bisexual or homosexual?

The Oracle then posed the question; "What then is the purpose of sexuality, if it is not solely for the purpose of reproduction? If sexuality is only for the reproduction of the individual involved, then where does homosexuality come from? For if reproduction was the sole purpose would not homosexuality have been eradicated from the gene pool." As shown above, contrary to popular opinion homosexuality exists throughout the animal kingdom. To use Darwinian logic for homosexuality to exist in nature there must be some survival value attached to it or else it would disappear as a behavior. If homosexuality exists not for the survival of the individual then it must somehow have survival value for the species. What could that be?

Surely then there must be more to sex in all its forms than merely reproduction? It seemed that the more the seeker learned about sexuality the more questions he had. Why did human introduce morality and judgment to sexuality? How could some humans perceive such widespread, well established homosexual behavior as unnatural when it exists so commonly in the animal kingdom? Could it be that the purpose of sex in addition to reproduction is also to strengthen the pair bond? If that were not so would not the sex drive disappear after the reproductive years have ended? The seeker could not help but notice that the world was filled with happy geriatrics that enjoyed copulating long after they had ceased having offspring. In addition lots of fertile couples willingly chose not to have children. They still copulated. Sex for them was and is a means of cementing their relationship, the pair bonding. If a married couple due to choice or infertility had no children, are they then less valuable as human beings? Are not great artists, great musicians, great philosophers, valuable to the human race? If they were homosexual are they somehow less valuable to the human race? Of course not! Homosexuality exists in all walks of life, and in many different species. It simply is part of nature's plan. It is not a moral construct but a natural one. Homosexuals contribute as much to the quality of life of as do heterosexuals and thereby contribute to the survival of the species. ***The primary purpose of sex is the survival of the species through the strengthening of the pair bond.*** To say that the love between a homosexual pair is somehow unnatural and inferior to the love between a heterosexual pair is ridiculous. Unconditional love is unconditional. It is not acceptable to love someone in spite of what they are. That is conditional. If love is to be unconditional, we must love someone because of what they are. "Love thy neighbor as thyself" is unconditional. Nowhere does it say "Love thy neighbor as thyself if."

Touching

In Nature's varied vast domain
No greater power than touch remains
No matter what the species be
Be it on the land, or in the sea.

In the human realm we must admit
That touching or the lack of it,
Sends out a message loud and clear
That without the touch we disappear

The caring touch, well placed in time,
Restores the Reason and the Rhyme,
Makes wounded hearts and spirits soar,
From winter's chill the warmth restore.

There's nothing kills a lover's song,
Like the icy chill of a touch withdrawn.
With shoulders cold, and empty eyes,
We chill the air with silent cries.

Successful lovers know this much.
They know the power of the touch.
They know the more and more you give,
The more you have, the more you live.

If all the world this understand,
Forget the difference, extend a hand
No spoken words need there be,
For all crave the Touch, like you and me.

Spooning

To cuddle close, to be as one.
To blend until the borders done
Like eclipsing sun to crescent moon
Back to front we lover's spoon.

Like placenta to womb apply
Blending skin, thigh to thigh
Heart to heart, skin to skin
Unlock the treasures that lie within.

Like wrapping vine around the tree,
Your thighs and arms do suckle me.
Melting hearts and minds in tune
Twin our souls beneath the moon.

In all of nature spooning scene
In great and small, it's loves routine.
We seek the comfort that closeness brings
That nectar makes the spirit sing.

When touch is there, we need no voice,
To speak the love that lies within.
Each others shadow we become,
Mind and bodies blend as one,

Our universe then lies within.
As our web of love we lovers spin.
A single thought consumes the mind,
That here we spoon till the end of time.

Smiles

I wore a Smile the other day, it stretched from ear to ear.
I smiled at everything I saw. I showed it everywhere . . .
The more I gave the more I got, a wondrous sight to see
And soon I found that deep inside the smile was changing me.

The smile I gave was returned, returned without conditions.
It seemed like magic, the effect it had, on people's dispositions.
A happy smile you cannot stop, it spread infectiously.
The magic power of the smile changed all that I could see.

So simple then the magic smile, a gift from deep inside;
A gift that keeps on coming back, from its journey far and wide.
It changes every place it's been. It changes us inside.
A smile can simply take us on a magic carpet ride.

A simple smile can lift the heart, weighed down with all its pain.
A magic gift that you can give, yet always can retain.

Chapter XI

"THE WISDOM OF CHILDREN"

As he had so often done before, during one of his extraneous meditation sessions the Oracle decided to make another visit to planet Earth, one of the places he frequented as he travelled the Cosmos in search of knowledge. Planet Earth, like his own had started out as a place where life was a lot simpler, with small villages and a greater concept of peace and brotherhood. Both were idealistic places, virtual utopias. Both were Gardens of Eden, however as millennia passed, villages grew into towns, towns grew into cities. Now there were counties, states, countries, languages, religions, wars, killings, intolerance. No longer driven by the search for knowledge, as once it had been in the days of Eden, the prime motivators of both lands had now become greed and power. The seeker believed that a lot could be learned about pain and suffering from the people on earth. It was different here. Here there was death. Not so, initially on Perpetua, now it was changing. Wanting to learn more about death and its effects on the living, the Oracle decided to visit one of the educational symposia on the planet earth taking about "How Children Perceive Death". The question of the day was: "What good, if any, could come from the death of a child?" He decided to listen in.

Best Mommy in the Whole World

To the people gathered at the forum on parenting, at first glance it seems that such a prospect was ludicrous given that the death of a child is such a catastrophic event. "Goodness in death; Preposterous!" Few could see any goodness and many were visibly upset at even the suggestion that there was any good there. A young parent stepped forward and pronounced to the gathering: "I have a story to tell; if you are willing to listen and you may judge for yourselves". He took the stage.

"Recently our youngest child Alexander, a healthy baby, died at the age of three months from SIDS. Sudden Infant Death Syndrome, he explained, was a poorly understood medical condition. It usually affects male children under six months of age. On the night of his death, our son Alexander was placed in his crib by me. He was placed on his stomach, now known as a definite risk factor but not then."

He went on to say. "I'll never forget that night. I burped Alexander after his supper and placed him in his crib, and went downstairs into the basement where I had my office. Alexander was our youngest of four children. Our oldest Jonathan was just turning six at the time, Rebecca was four and Nathan nearly three. Alexander was a very healthy 8 lb 12 ounce baby at birth. He was never sick and did not have a blemish on his body. It was October 30th and in every way it was a normal night. Having fed and burped Alexander, while his mother was doing the dishes, I placed him in his crib, which was the type that swung back and forth. I forgot to lock the crib and with hindsight I wonder if that carelessness in any way contributed to Alex's death."

"Somehow Alex managed to work himself into the corner and was found there by my wife one hour later, mottled, not breathing, and with no pulse. I was downstairs when I heard my wife screaming as she came into my office carrying the baby in her arms. Immediately I knew what had happened as the baby looked mottled. I screamed "Oh my Jesus! Crib Death" I started CPR on Alex but after 40 minutes or so it called it off because the baby was showing no sign of recovery. I won't go through the thoughts that were racing through my head at this point in the story, but suffice it to say that calling off the CPR was the toughest decision I have ever had to make. The consequences of that decision would not be revealed for five more years.

The morning after Alexander's death, my wife's family arrived to help us in our moment of tragedy with the kids and other activities of daily living. Mary, her sister, helped us get the kids ready for Halloween and tried to make daily life decisions with them. Jonathan and Rebecca had been informed that Alexander had gone to Heaven but we were not sure if they fully comprehended the situation. This fact was of great concern to us, until the next morning when the good that comes out of death occurred. For I firmly believe that there is some good to be found in every bad.

On Halloween night my wife's sister Mary had taken the kids to bed with her and read stories to them. The second morning after Alexander's death I went into the kid's room to see how they were doing. Mary had the kids laughing as she read them a story. It was then that the magic moment occurred, a moment that I will never forget, a moment in which you know that your kids will be alright. This magic moment was a message from heaven to heal the soul. I had been feeling very proud of my wife for the strength that she was showing in our grief, exuding the qualities of courage and clarity of thought that made me love her so much, she was nurturing and consoling the many visitors who shared our grief and had come to console us. Feeling proud, with teary eyes I went upstairs to visit the kids. I opened the door. The kids were playing on the bed with their auntie Mary. With pride in my voice I told the children that they had "the best mommy in the whole world." To my surprise my eldest son Jonathan, age six, replied in a loud voice, *No We Don't*. Not believing my ears I said *What* and Jonathan's next reply left me with a feeling of pride, comfort and amazement. For with wisdom far beyond his six years he said words I'll never forget; he said "We don't have the best mommy in the whole world because, **Every mommy is the best mommy in the whole world**"!

His voice filled with emotion, the young man paused to take a sip of water He was about to relate how his son Alexander's death had affected his youngest son Nathan.

Impressed by what he heard the Oracle decided to continue to listen to the fascinating story that the young man was telling to the captivated assembly. He continued.

NATHAN AND ANNE OF GREEN GABLES

"Nathan was only three years old when his baby brother Alexander, age three months, died of a SIDS death. It was hard to predict the impact that such a momentous event would have on such a young mind. Even before Alexander's death, Nathan was a challenge, always getting in trouble. It seemed like he was always fighting with Jonathan and Rebecca and we always had to punish him for something. The full impact of Alexander's death became glaringly obvious to us nine months later, when we were all in Prince Edward Island watching the play 'Anne of Green Gables'.

"Nathan was always a competitive kid. He was the third child of four and raised hell all the time. Jonathan age six, Rebecca age five were very close and got along extremely well. Nathan, being the new kid on the block, was always competing for his place in the sun and got his attention by being an "Anti-Christ" as we say in Newfoundland.

Jonathan seemed not to change with Alexander's death but it was much different for Nathan. Jonathan and Rebecca were very close, Nathan being the third child always felt left out. The only way he could get attention, he thought, was by being bad. Then along came Alexander the fourth child, and took away even more of his mother's attention. As a result it seemed like Nathan had a love-hate relationship with Alexander."

About two days before Alexander died Nathan gave Alexander a bite on the arm. He did not leave a mark but the mere fact that he did it showed his resentment for those that would steal his mother's attention from him. His grandmother scolded Nathan and told him that if he continued to bite Alex, Alex would be taken away. Two days later Alexander died. We did not know what grandma had said until later, and did not realize the impact that such an innocent remark would have on Nathan until nine months later in Prince Edward Island.

After Alexander's death Nathan became very withdrawn. He would still raise hell but stopped biting. Nathan however continued to give us grief. We did not know what to do. He just kept getting punished."

Nathan had never cried when Alexander died, but his acting out continued to get worse. The true depth of the impact of Alexander's death on Nathan became painfully obvious when the family was vacationing in P.E. I. We had gone to see Anne of Green Gables. We were sitting five in a row, in the third row back from the stage. The theatre was packed. At the scene, when the character Matthew was dying, the theatre fell deadly silent. Nathan had left his seat and had crawled into his mother's arms. Suddenly the silence was broken by loud sobs and crying. The tormented words from a child, like a voice in Hell, rang in my ears. The child was sobbing uncontrollably: "He's not coming back! He's not coming back!" It was Nathan."

The gift of a child is the gift of knowledge not yet revealed.
PJ Morry 2012

PARENTS IN TROUBLE

With a quivering voice and fighting back tears the young father continued his presentation to the conference. *"Alexander's death not only profoundly affected the children it profoundly affected my wife and I. We did not know it at the time, but Alexander's death would have repercussions for years to come.* Initially we were drawn together trying to heal each other's pain but eventually his death became a wedge between us. We dealt with our grief in different ways, and we drew further apart. My wife went into a deep depression that I did not fully appreciate. I was able to lose myself in my work. If I seemed to heal faster than she; she would get angry. She would scream at me. "How could you forget so easily?" She had lost her baby, she felt she had lost herself. Always the nurturer, she had now become angry, nothing could console her; black was white, white was black. It seemed that she was beyond consolation. I could do nothing right, and I withdrew into my work. We argued all the time over nothing and over everything. Worse that the arguments were the silences, silences so loud they were deafening.

Two years later, my wife could still be seen pressing Alexander's pajamas to her face. She swore that she could still smell him. That sweet baby scent that only a mother could appreciate was everywhere. At times I thought I could smell it. I tried at times when she was not around. Perhaps I could but I wasn't sure, But she could smell him, of that there was no doubt. Her memory of his scent would never leave her. How unloving of me to have forgotten it! Not being a mother I did not understand and it made her angry. After all I put him down. I forgot to lock the crib. I could not revive him. We never spoke about it. But it was there, every minute, every day. When we did speak we walked on egg shells above a pit of verbal barbs. Our relationship was dying the death of a thousand knives." We tried to have another child hoping that would somehow ease the pain, but my wife had had a tubal ligation and we had to resort to "Invetro Fertilization". Three times it did not work. It was an emotional roller coaster ride to Hell and back. The hormones played havoc with my wife, bringing back the pain every time the procedure failed. Building up her hopes, and then dashing them. Another baby would not bring back Alexander but it might bring her back from her own private hell.

A turning point came one evening when we were watching a TV show at home. My wife was sitting on the couch between me and the TV. I could only see her profile. We were watching a show about a four year old girl who had fallen through the ice on a river. She had been completely submersed in water over her head for 30 minutes before rescue. When she was found, she had no pulse, was extremely hypothermic and was not breathing. Miraculously she recovered and with little or no detectable brain damage. A miracle! I looked at my wife, she was silent. She would not look at me. I stared at the back of her head silhouetted by the TV Screen. There was a long silence. I asked her, "Are you thinking what I think you're thinking?" Still there was no answer. She continued to look at the screen saying nothing. "You're thinking I quit resuscitating Alexander too early aren't you?" I asked, knowing but not wanting to hear the answer. "Her response filled with anger and pain was hesitant icy cold, and barely audible. A single word, barely audible, and sharp as a knife, shattered the icy air between us and left me numb. "Yes!"

My poor wife had spoken the unspeakable. She had harbored for five years the belief that not only had I placed our child, her child, in the crib and maybe contributed to his death by failing to lock the crib, but that I had failed to resuscitate him. She believed all this time that I had stopped the resuscitation too early. She thought that I had given up too early on our child, on Alexander! For years this unthinkable belief had haunted her, had filled her with pain and ambivalence, and had prevented her from healing. She expressed her anger in a thousand ways. She had thought the unthinkable, but could not speak the unspeakable. Not wanting to hurt her husband by voicing her doubts, she silently tried to bury the unbearable thought but it would not go away. The quiet way in which she said "yes" was like a thunder bolt. For the first time I really understood how devastating Alexander's death had been and how little I had appreciated my wife's pain."

We decided to get counseling."

ALEXANDER

A Mother's dream, this newborn child, A Universe held in protective arms,
Purity, unblemished still, all nature yields to his seductive charms.
How can it be this wondrous thing, can mountains move and souls inspire?
How can it be those sparkling eyes, can consume all hearts with such a fire?

This little gift from Gods own grace, can all the care and pain erase

This infant with the gentle smile, and skin so soft, all hearts beguile
With gentle ease, and quiet peace, a child can still the raging beast,
This tiny child, so unaware of all his power, lying there.

And yet, with piercing of the heart, to knowing God all souls depart.
And why the Father of the Sun (Son], hath stole this young life just begun?
To crib this child was laid by me, to rest for all eternity.
I did not know that it would be, that God would take my world from me.

These words "I lay thee down to sleep, and pray the Lord thy soul to keep".
Keep safe, protect from evils there, while child you sleep so unaware.
This prayer so cruel, now never say, for God has taken you away,
Just three months old my baby be, when God took you away from me.

T'is bitter sweet the pain I live, for Life is God's to take or give.
All life truly springs from thee, though sometimes all to brief it be.
I had you for a little while, this miracle that was my child.
Precious Memories, thought few they be, a gift that God did give to me.

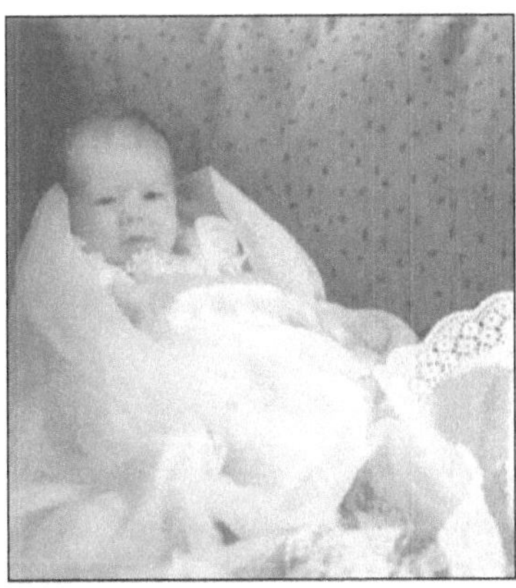

Baby Alexander Christening

On loan

"I'll lend you for a little time,
a child of mine," God said;
"For you to love the while he lives,
and mourn for when he's dead.
It may be four or five years,
or twenty-two or three
but will you, 'till I call him back
Take care of him for me?

He'll bring his charms to gladden you,
and shall his stay be brief
you'll have his lovely memories,
as solace for your grief

I cannot promise he will stay,
Since all from earth return
But there are lessons taught down there,
I want this child to learn
I've looked the wide world over
In my search for teachers true,
And from the throngs that crowd life's lane,
I have selected you,
Now will you give him all your love,
not think the labor vain,
nor hate me when I come
to take him back again?

I fancied that I heard them say:
'Dear Lord, Thy will be done!
For all the joy Thy child shall bring,
the risk of grief we'll run.
We'll shelter him while we may,
And for all the happiness we've known,
forever grateful stay.
But shall the angels call him
much sooner than we've planned,
we'll brave the bitter grief that comes,
and surely understand.'

Written in 1988 by Tara Marie Parker from North Carolina.
It was written for a friend that died and presented to her parents

Chapter XII

"PARENTING"

On Perpetua there was no death, so the Oracle on his journey to Earth decided to check out a maternity ward. He decided to fly over a hospital on his way to a Symposium he had heard about. The topic was 'The Meaning of Death'. On Perpetua the arrival of a new life was not of great significance to the seekers. Tired of existing in one form a seeker would simply change into another form. On Perpetua there was no birth, no death. There was only transformation and renewal. On earth humans viewed death as an ending, and birth as a beginning. Death and birth were always topics of great debate amongst scholars, philosophers and clerics. On earth, the seeker was to find out that the birth of a child was a matter of great celebration. He decided to check it out.

Holding the newborn baby, the proud parents could not contain their joy. They had been blessed with a beautiful baby girl. They had called her Emma. The gift of a new beginning filled with promise had been bestowed upon them. Not only was this a new beginning for the child, but a new beginning for the parents, for as parents their lives would never be the same. Now they will become nurturers, providers, and protectors. They will become teachers and most importantly students, as they acquire the gifts of; compassion, understanding, patience, and most importantly love. Their dilemmas will be many, their choices hard. How much freedom is too much? How much too little? Do I let them make their own mistakes; or do I protect them? What is the right amount of discipline; of freedom? How do parents know if they made the right choice? How will their success be measured? The journey through the mine field of parenting would be the most challenging and rewarding adventure of the young parent's lives. At times, the responsibilities would stress their relationship. At times it would be the glue that held it together. They would learn lessons from their children that would give them wisdom and grow their love. Through their children they would get to know themselves and would get to know God. Their children, who at birth would know nothing, would teach them everything.

Roots and Wings

I plant this tree, this tiny tree. What will it be?
Where will I plant it, in the shade of another tree?
Protected from the wind, rain and sun?
Smothered in shadows? Withered before it has begun!

Or will I plant it near, but not too far away,
Where it can be nurtured by the light of day.
Alone! Will it die? Or, will it rocket to the sky?
Seeking its own place, racing its neighbor's to birds that fly.

You'll have your winds, your storms, your rains!
Your cloudy days, your growing pains!
Never smothered by parental fears of letting go.
Your trunk is strong. Your roots are deep.
You're free to grow.

So little tree, I'll give thee space.
With roots and wings, you'll win the race.
Your inner strength will set you free,
And inspire all who look on thee.

"Sharing"

On his flight over Brigus, Newfoundland, the Oracle observed a crowd of people on their way to watch some fireworks at the music festival. He was intrigued by a three generation family walking along the road. The grandfather had taken his entire family to the Music Festival. The three year old granddaughter was watching all the other children running around with all sorts of sparkles and artificial lights. Everyone was going to the ocean to see the fireworks. The Grandfather had heard that it would be awesome and was excited to share this experience with his granddaughter, Emma who was riding on his shoulders. Hundreds of people of all ages excitedly hurried along. Emma, while riding on her poppa's shoulders had noticed that some children had lights that were really tall and flashed many colors and she really wanted one. Emma was distraught when she was informed that they were all sold out, however, a little girl nearby, who had two of the lights, noticed Emma's distress, and generously offered Emma one of her two lights. Emma, of course, was delighted and gladly accepted one of the lights.

Being a good grandparent, the grandfather took the opportunity to teach his Emma all about the joys of sharing. He thanked the little girl that had shared her flashing light with them, and proceeded to praise the act of sharing by saying, "see Emma sharing is good". Poppa was happy and felt very proud that he taught a valuable lesson to Emma, however his pride and happiness was short-lived. Still on her Poppas shoulders, as they walked towards the ocean, with people all around, Emma noticed another little girl with two flashing lights and she herself still had only one. Emma called out in a bold and loud voice "Hey little girl, little girl, little girl, until finally the little girl looked up at Emma riding on her poppas shoulders. When Emma finally realized that the little girl was listening she boldly exclaimed: "Little girl! Sharing is good!

"Oh the joys of parenting"!

Chapter XIII

"THE AWAKENING"

The Oracle had hardly finished laughing at the wiles of the little girl when his consciousness was pierced by the agonizing cries of a young man whose pain had travelled around the globe. The young man whose name was Brad was hopelessly lost and despondent.

Brad was a dedicated missionary. Filled with the desire to help the needy he had used his church to fill that need and was posted to Costa Rica where for twenty years he faithfully performed his tasks of ministering to the needy. It seemed that every waking hour was spent caring for others. He was their pastor, their teacher, at times their doctor. He was there to advocate for his peoples every need. He served on the village council, wrote letters to government, and raised money through charities for local causes. His wife was left to raise their five children plus do all the repairs to their home, tend to the crops and animals and manage the home finances. He hardly spent any time at home and one day she complained to him that "he would step over her to get to a client" He mistakenly took that as a compliment! The harder he worked it seemed the worse things got. She feeling neglected started to withdraw. They had little time for relaxation and even less for intimacy, in fact there was none.

Brad confused and hurt, and was conflicted by the love/ hate relationship he had with his wife. For years they had struggled. He worked so hard to be a good provider. Too hard it seems, because they had little time for play and argued about everything. In his youthful arrogance he was convinced that she did not understand him and the importance of his work. He in turn did not see that she too had given her all, but only saw that *he was slaving away*. He had poured his heart and soul into his work, was consumed by it. He did not see his own faults. He did not see his own mistakes. Nor did he recognize the tremendous contribution his wife had given to the relationship. He only saw that she had become cold and withdrawn. It was not always that way. Once there was fire and passion. What had happened?

Feeling unhappy and neglected Brad began looking for answers outside. He had an affair, which made him feel worse. When he told his wife she asked him to leave. Not wanting to leave and still not looking inside he went to a councilor to help him fix his wife. Needless to say, since he was looking in the wrong places, things did not improve.

Soon the pain became unbearable and the relationship nearly terminal. He did not know where to turn. Exhausted he fell asleep. The Oracle inserted himself into the Brad's dream and took him on a journey of self discovery, across the sea of confusion, up the mountain of pain across the lake of hope to the island of wisdom so that he might drink from the *Fountain of Knowledge.*

With his heart heavy and full of pain Brad met with oracle and explained how after all his years of hard work and dedication everything was falling apart. He did not realize that his wife was that unhappy. He always thought that she was OK with him, that she had the same goals as he did. He did not ask her what she wanted, she would always be there. He thought the problems they were having were serious but not urgent and could be fixed later. He was beginning to realize that he did not understand her and for sure he thought that she did not understand him.

The oracle listened patiently for long time while the man poured out his heart. His face washed with tears, and every tear thundered when it hit the floor leadened with the weight of the pain therein. The oracle listened and listened and said nothing. Finally exhausted the young man fell to the floor drained and still confused. The oracle told him to drink from the fountain of knowledge and then to bath in the lake of hope and after three days of fasting and meditation to come back. He was instructed that when he did come back he was to tell his story again this time in the form of poetry for the oracle knew that poetry helps clear the mind of feeling that put up walls and hide the truth.

As he departed the Oracle told him three things to help guide his thinking: (1) "You only get one chance to be a family; (2) the grass is not greener on the other side of the fence. **The grass is greenest on the side you water**"; (3) and finally, "He who looks outside . . . . . . dreams. **He who looks inside . . . . awakens**!" *Carl Jung*

With hope in his heart and an open mind the young man set off to drink from the fountain of knowledge, bath in the lake of hope, fast and meditate.

The Telling Time

No tender Heart do I see
But a soul that craves security
No Passion there, but only fear
From deadly wounds of yesteryear.

No after play, No be as one
She rests assured, her duty done.
I lie there empty, unwrapped, undone
Await the touch that does not come.

I try small touches just to see, what response they bring.
Will you come close, and tender be, and cuddle in?
Will precious words I long to hear,
Be softly whispered, "I love you dear"?

Will gentle smiles free of care, my eyes caress?
Will gentle moans and whispers dear, my heart impress?
Will precious moments packed with love, Time suspend,
And make those empty lonely longing feelings end?

Coupling done, the first few seconds tell it all.
This telling time! Will I soar? Will I fall?
If touch happens in that time, I will fly.
If nothing does, the time too long, Again I die.

I wait and Wait and Wait, my spirit falls
There is no touch, no word, No none at all!
Dash those Dreams! My heart screams out,
Put up your WALLS! Get out and do your business calls!

Her duty done, asleep she lies so unaware
Of the confused and bitter hurt, raging near.
Another wedge, another brick put in my wall.
Next time I know I'll have less far to fall.

Until the day, not far away, when I'll not fly.
Apart we'll be, behind our WALLS and wonder why.
The feeling gone, No tender touch to await
We do our duty, when time is long, and fornicate.

"The grass is greenest on the side you water". These words resonated within the young man. If you treasure something you nurture it. So simple! So easily forgotten!

The Awakening

For years I slaved towards the light.
Climbed the ladder of success.
I toiled, and climbed, and fought the night
In search of happiness.

Along the way you were there,
Working by my side
Focused obsessed and unaware
I pushed you far aside.

I drove myself so hard it seems
I had no time at all
No time to look and see that I
Had climbed a different wall.

The wall I climbed had little gain
The fight was ill begun.
Anger, disappointment, pain
Were prizes I had won.

Alone I climbed so hard and long
Alone and unaware
The wall I climbed was over here
And you were over there

For all that was near and dear to me
I readily threw aside
Forgot that what's important
Is the journey and the ride

For life is what happens while we're
Busy making plans.
Don't look to see where we must go
No time to understand.

Thank God I know, I've been a fool
I hope it's not too late
Take time to let my engines cool
Take time to meditate.

With love we can bridge the gap
That exists between our WALLS.
And flow with spring's eternal sap
Towards heaven's hallowed halls

Three days of fasting and meditation had enabled Brad to get in touch with his feelings through his poetry. The healing power of enlightenment had released a torrent of tears of pain. Like a flash flood in a thunderstorm, the torrent of tears flooded his desiccated, shriveled spirit nurturing his newly planted seeds of hope. As he looked long within, his own role in the failures of his relationship was revealed, and the murky waters of confusion that hid the truth were slowly clearing. The words of the oracle echoed in his head "He who looks outside . . . . dreams; He who looks inside awakens?" He had a lot of fixing to do! He had a lot of grass to water and it was going to take a long time to get it green again, but it would happen. It was just a matter of time. "You only get one chance to be a family!"

Little Things Mean a Lot

The tender touch, the loving stare, the eyes that say, you forever care,
The gentle hug, the tender kiss, all keeps our love both young and fresh.

Too oft we cease those little things, the bread that makes the spirit sing.
Go on our way and do ignore the things that make our spirits soar.

We do our deeds, both great and small. We fill our days and don't recall
That in our youth, T'was little things, that made our hearts and spirits sing.

The old must to the young return, to find the truth and message learn
That t'is the gift of little things, that make our hearts and spirits sing.

Brad's demons had been released leaving him drained but not empty. For now his spirit filled with hope and a new love. A more intense and mature love filled his soul, a love without conditions, an unselfish love, a forgiving love. Love was all powerful. He knew that all he needed was love, for love was everything. His persona had changed, he stood tall. An aura radiated from his body that was visible to all. He had been purified.

He returned to the oracle, but did not need to speak. The oracle could see the transformation and knew that his words to the seeker had been heard and understood. ***"He who looks outside dreams . . . He who looks inside . . . . awakens".***

Carl Jung

Chapter XIV

THE POWER OF FORGIVENESS

Please help me I'm drowning

This can't be real. There must be more. All I feel is pain
I'm sinking to the ocean floor never to rise again.
The fading light is far away, getting dimmer by the minute.
The inky blackness of my pain drowns everything within it.
Deeper deeper down I go. I'll never make it back.
The fading light that was my home now is just a speck.
My lungs are bursting with my pain. My soul is filled with dread.
I'll never see the light again, for soon I will be dead.
Just let it out! Just exhale! Soon it all will end.
Death, sweet death you must not fear. He truly is a friend.
Just drift away, from the day, the day that was your hell,
Into the darkness of the night, where torment does not dwell!
Will I kick my legs and try to swim, or slowly drift on down?
Just open wide, let death inside; your peace is all around.

Do not fear; you're nearly there.

Let out the air.

Let out the air.

Just let it out!

Deep in the Canadian wilderness the Oracle saw a lonely man in a canoe, who remained motionless for what seemed like an eternity. He looked distraught, as the Oracle watched the man lean over his canoe staring into the jet black, deathly, still foreboding waters of the mountain lake which mirrored the empty void that was inside him. As he stared at his own reflection, he saw the void that was his soul. The Oracle read his thoughts. "It would be so easy to end it here; just lean, just a little and my pain and my shame would end. How did it come to this"? He had been a young physician, dedicated, considered a good candidate for winning the *Practice of Excellence Award,* and now he was disgraced. For sixteen years he had toiled in the town of his birth; the town where he practiced as a young physician determined to be the best that there ever was. He had three children, a beautiful supporting wife; a beautiful ocean front home nestled against barrier reefs that were continuously shrouded in thundering waves and mist. He had everything; had given everything; and now he felt drained.

He stared into the black cold water for what seemed like an eternity deep in thought. It could be all over in just a few minutes, but then the truth would never be known. He would remain disgraced and worse yet would likely be considered a coward by his children who still believed in him. He had to redeem himself. He had to show the world that he was not capable of doing that; that for which he was accused. That horrible foreign act, the thought of which almost made him vomit, was the antithesis of everything he was. He was nurturing, caring, loving, and compassionate. He could never abuse, particularly sexual, it disgusted him. It was true that in his moment of confusion, desperation, isolation, and loss of his dream he had done the unthinkable, he had had an affair, but abuse Never!

Determined to erase this abhorrent accusation from the minds of all who knew him; he decided he must not die, not now, not this way. Slowly with tormented mind and heavy heart he paddled his canoe to the shore.

The previous sixteen years were busy, the hectic pace numbing. Consumed with a sense of responsibility and a desire for excellence, he had neglected the one most important thing of all, he had neglected to smell the roses. Not enough time for family, for nurturing, for relaxation, had taken its toll. He had estranged the person he cared for most in the world: the mother of his children, his companion, his friend, his wife, his compass.

The years of hard work in his native town had brought him to a state of near collapse. When he heard an ambulance, a police siren, or even the phone ring he would be filled with a deep dread of anticipation. Every waking moment was focused on his responsibilities as a physician. He could not let go. He could not turn off the switch. Occasionally he vomited blood. For sixteen years he had been on call 24/7. He had at one point worked a period of four years without a week off. Patients came to his home day and night with one emergency or another. He rarely got a chance to sit down to Christmas dinner without interruption. He rarely got to go to his kid's school concerts without being called away. He did not go off into the wilderness with his children fishing, and was hardly ever out of reach of a cell phone in case of an emergency call. Everybody knew him and everybody expected special treatment. He never knew how to say no. He recalled a blustery winter Sunday morning when he was about to take his 10 year old son to his Atom hockey game at the arena which was forty kilometers away. Just as he was about to leave a car arrived with a man with a cut finger. Not having the courage to say "no I cannot do it, you must go to emergency", the young physician gave the man four stitches and bandaged the man's finger. Now because he was running late and his son stood a chance of missing most of his hockey game he drove to the arena at unsafe speeds. When he was about one / half way there he told his son to take off his seat belt, get in the back and put his hockey gear so that he could go on the ice right away. His son complied and by the time they arrived at the arena he was crying and vomiting. He had been tossed around in the back seat as the vehicle careened down the highway sometimes on two wheels. In addition his son had missed the first period. The father did not realize at the time that he had put his sons' life at risk because he couldn't say no to a patient with a minor cut.

Finally, he decided to move away from his idyllic home. He needed to abandon his dream of living there forever. He moved as far away as he could, seven thousand kilometers, initially leaving his wife and children in the home that he loved. It was there, even more isolated from all that mattered, that he had had an affair. Brief, unsatisfying, emptying, it served only to make him feel worse.

Two weeks after he had ended his affair he was accused of assault. The weeks following the charges were his weeks of greatest shame. The police had formally charged him *with administering a noxious substance and sexual assault.* His good work to date had allowed the police to extend to him a small mercy which may have saved his life given his current mental state; they did not arrest him handcuffed, in front of the TV cameras etc., but had allowed him to come in at a predetermined time under his own recognizance. He was fingerprinted, formally charged and advised not to travel outside the country. His passport was confiscated. Adding to his shame and humiliation, the newspapers and T V stations were filled with the story. He stopped reading the papers and stopped watching TV. He could not even read the charges against him; they were so horrible and so against his nature. They were cruel unspeakable distortions. Everyone, everywhere, even back in his hometown knew about his shame. He was ashamed to speak to anyone, ashamed to go outside. He especially felt ashamed to talk to his own mother who thankfully was so far away. His mother was once was so proud of her son, the doctor. What now? In the middle of all this his mother died. Just before her death she had gone into a deep depression herself and had wished she was dead. She got her wish. She had a stroke. For days on end the young physician cried like a baby.

He again thought of killing himself. Two things stopped him. He could not do that to his children. They still believed he was innocent. *He was innocent! Now he must prove it, it was a matter of life and death. He must not go to prison.* He would die in prison, he knew it.

When the investigation was completed, after what seemed like an eternity, all the charges were stayed. He had been vindicated. However he was not completely innocent for he had broken a major rule and had dishonored his profession. He had had a relationship with a patient. This battle would be harder to win because this time he was guilty, and as a physician he had to deal with his governing body the College of Physicians and Surgeons. He had to be punished. He was suspended for one year.

The year of disgrace was a difficult one. He was not allowed to practice medicine and could not afford to travel. He became a recluse. His shame hung over him like a cloud. He wanted to be invisible. He felt like he was wearing a fluorescent red robe of shame in a world of black and white. The burning stain of shame, like acid in an open wound, prevented any healing. He would need a thorough cleansing. The year was an eternity.

Fortunately for him his wife and family had joined him. Times were difficult. Wounds were deep. A relationship deeply in trouble was now near dead. His shame was also hers. All his children were hurting but his eldest son a sensitive child of thirteen was struggling. His father had wounded him badly. His son was ashamed of him. His father was no longer his hero; the love/ hate feelings in his son's heart tore him apart. He withdrew into his own world of shame.

For the young physician, the veil of shame followed him everywhere he went. It was there in every breath, in every gaze, there when he got up, there when he went to sleep, there when he was in a crowd, and there when he was alone. His shame was so heavy it was suffocating. He could not escape. He could not cry. There were no more tears. He had fallen, fallen, fallen into a deep depression. He was dead. In fact he was worse than dead, for when you are dead you feel nothing. He was in Hell.

How could he begin to heal the deep wound he had inflicted on himself and those he loved the most? One day, deep in thought, while getting groceries at the corner store a good heart noticed his despair. This stranger ***put his hand on the young physicians shoulder*** and simply said "We believe in you. You will be *alright*". Those simple words ***"we believe in you"*** were words from his redeemer, were words straight from God. This stranger had given the young physician the gift of forgiveness. Instinctively, the physician knew that in time, if he believed in himself, others would believe in him and things would be alright.

The road would be hard and long. The scars were thick, and deep. Remarkably through all of this his wife was still with him. He knew that she was staying only for the children. He had broken her heart. He had hurt a lot of people. He had been forgiven by a stranger. Now he had to be forgiven by his wife. That would be harder to achieve. He had read something somewhere that would become his motto for the rest of his life, and would guide him on the long difficult path ahead. ***"Honor is a gift you give yourself. No one can give it to you and no one can take it from you."*** His path was clear, his journey long, but he would be alright.

Forgiveness

Furry four legged friend of man
You've done what no other creature can
Companion, friend, now by man's side
Ten Thousand years, you do reside.

What is the secret laying there?
Of this communion so unfair!
For man who is so hard to please,
You little doggie you do with ease.

Relationships seldom seem to be
From now until eternity.
For those of us with fight concerned,
There is a lesson to be learned.

Cruel, neglect, disdain, we show.
And yet the doggie loves us so.
I feel the secret is released
In the forgiving nature of the beast.

If mankind, others could forgive
In Peace, respect, could learn to live.
If husband wife could turn their head

And forget that ugly words were said.
Forgive, forget like doggies do
And love without a string or two
How simple then life it would be
For forgiving folks like you and me.

Chapter XV

LOVE AND TRUTH

As they continued on their journey around planet Earth in their search for knowledge the Oracle and Bill came upon a middle aged woman sitting on a rock watching the ocean waves crashing on the shore. She had a bottle of wine half finished and she was listening to her favorite song on her headset. The song she was listening to was "One and only" by Adele; she was sobbing uncontrollably. The Oracle took the fatherly form of an old fisherman and approached her. He showed her a seashell he had picked up on the beach and handed it to her. When she accepted it she felt a strange feeling of peace envelope her and she felt safe. She usually avoided people and was not accustomed to looking into people's faces, but she was drawn to his and when she looked in his eyes she felt his spirit flow into her. She felt calm and strangely aware of her feelings that were no longer those of shame and torment but of acceptance. He asked her why she was crying. She told him her story.

That day, her mother who had developed Alzheimer's, had for the first time forgotten her name. Her mother could not remember her own daughter's name. Her name! It was a startling realization. She smiled sadly and related the fact that at birth she had kicked up such a fuss that her mother had called her "Gale" and now her own mother did not even know who she was. To make matters worse, her father had yet again reinforced her own feelings of inadequacy and failure when he repeated the words that were like a knife in her heart, "how can someone so smart be so stupid?" She wanted so desperately to be loved and accepted by her father whom she worshipped. She wanted him to hold her and, just occasionally, hug her, but the hugs never came. She could not remember him ever saying he loved her. He had a great sense of humor and could make anyone laugh at even the simplest things, and yet that same deriding sense of humor in an instant could reduce her to tears and destroy her self confidence.

A bright girl with two University degrees, she felt a failure. Her father cruelly reminded her of all her mistakes and in her mind he never recognized any of her successes. Never having experienced hugs, kisses and acceptance for who she was, she fell in love with a man as cold as her father but who made her father appear saintly in comparison with the extent of his abuses. After 20 years of verbal abuse, physical abuse, she finally found the courage to pack her bags and leave with her two children. She left with no assets, no child support, nothing. The only thing she had was a small sense of pride on finally after 20 years working up the courage to leave this abusive person who had so totally crushed her spirit for all those years. She wanted to make it work but the abuse was too intense and now she was separated with nothing and a complete failure in her own eyes. With no money, no car, no assets, nothing she left her husband 2000 miles away and returned home to her parents. She was a failure. Her husband had told her that every day and now she had proved him right.

When Gale got home, instead of being supportive, her father reaffirmed that she couldn't do anything right. He called her a failure too. Three years later her father still would ask her almost daily when she was going to crawl back to her ex. She had gone into a depression, she cried every day, she provided for her kids, worked two jobs, but did not socialize. She did not date men, she was afraid of men. She did not believe that they could see anything in her. They would always want sex and she hated sex. Her husband had abused her for so long in so many ways. She felt so ugly and so dirty. The thought of sex would turn her to stone. It scared her, she never dated. Her kids were her life and they were almost grown up.

She used to write. Her degrees were in English and Education. She taught school once, had her own theater company but had lost all desire to interact with people. She had become a recluse. She did work that she could do in her room on her computer. She seldom left the house. Her dad was also showing some signs of Alzheimer's. She worried about them constantly. She felt powerless, cheated.

Nobody Wants to Keep Me

Everybody wants me, but no one wants to keep
me, she cried and wondered why.
Her sorrow honed by retreat as she watched the years roll by.
The blighted dreams of innocent youth, now chains both long and strong.
She wondered how it happened; how things could go so wrong.

The playful, laughing, smiling girl, that used to love the Play,
With fetal curl, and curtains drawn, now dreads the light of day.
This battered beauty cannot see, with broken lenses clearly.
Abusive husband for years has flown, yet still torments her daily.

Rejection, pain, distain, abuse were hers as years rolled past.
Her future furled, her body curled into her fetal past.
The future has become her past; their welded into one.
She dreads the light that gives her sight, into what she has become.

Suitors want her. She's had her share. They want but will not give.
They take and take, and almost break that fragile will to live.
The world outside, a nightmare ride that chills her to the bone.
She hides away and dreads the day, and makes her chair her home.

Her days are nights, her fear she fights, her morning has no sun.
From endless day she hides away. She has no place to run.
The only arms that hold her are the chair that traps her form.
Huddled there in her prison chair, the only safety that she's known.

Like a broken mirror piece by piece, she gave herself away.
She must protect the pieces left, so in her chair she'll stay.
The lesson learned, from the men concerned. She feels like pocket change.
Everyone wants her, but no one wants to keep her.

A Little Bit of Nothing

Once we loved each other. You were my light of day.
You consumed me with your fire, then you took your love away.
Now darkness drowns the sunshine. My skies are filled with rain.
Despair is now an ocean that floods my heart with pain.

Chorus
I've got a little bit of nothing,
And got nowhere to fall,
A little bit of nothing,
And afraid to lose it all.

A little bit of nothing, gets less as time goes by.
A little bit of nothing will bleed me till I die.
A little bit of nothing, more weight than I can bear.
A little bit of nothing; I see it everywhere.

A little bit of nothing, can flood my world with tears.
A little bit of nothing, can't wash away my fears.
A little bit of nothing, just a dream how things should be.
A little bit of nothing, is all you offer me.

Chorus
I've got a little bit of nothing
And got nowhere to fall,
A little bit of nothing,
And afraid to lose it all.

A little bit of nothing, our love has grown so small.
A little bit of nothing, is worse than none at all.
A little bit of nothing, got nowhere to fall,
A little bit of nothing, and afraid to lose it all.

Gale wasn't even sure she knew what love was. She asked the Oracle "What is love? She wanted it, she was afraid of it, and more afraid she might find it and lose it. She could not take another rejection. It would kill her.

WHAT IS LOVE?

The Oracle smiled at her, looked into her eyes and explained what he had learned about love in all his travels. He did not tell her he had been observing man for thousands of years. He spoke as a fisherman, a man who was in tune with himself and with his world. He revealed to her the following.

He said. "In my travels among the Innu, I made an interesting observation. The Innu had forty or more words for snow because there are so many different types of snow but yet in all the languages of the world there was only one word for love." The Oracle had wondered about that. There were so many adjectives to describe love; such as true love, unselfish love, pure love, young love, puppy love, old love, unrequited love, misguided love, wasted love, natural love, selfish love, unconditional love etc., yet there was only one word for love itself. As a result, when people spoke of love just as when people spoke of God, there was great potential for miscommunication and as a consequence misconception and hurt. And as with God, few people knew what love really was. They did not realize that perhaps love and God was actually the same thing. The Oracle advised the woman that love is a dangerous word and should be spoken only with great care. Sometimes the meaning is clearest when the word is not spoken at all, and yet people wanted to be told that they were loved and that in truth was where the problem lay. The Oracle observed that there may be a valid reason why there was only one word for love. Perhaps no one really knew what it really was; just like no one really knows what God is, or what time is. Perhaps, in reality love did not actually exist. It had no boundaries, it could not be measured. It had no weight; it did not occupy space; it was more than just an idea; more than just a feeling. In truth love can only exist as an action. It can only be seen and felt through action. Therefore telling someone you love them is both unnecessary and meaningless. It is about as important as telling your plants you love them! If you love your plants, you show them by your action. You water them.

"What is the greatest kind of love" the young woman asked?" "That one is simple" answered the Oracle: "Love of self is the greatest kind of love, because if you cannot love yourself, then how can you be expected to love somebody else?" The woman commented "Is not love of self, self-centered and narcissistic and thus to be discouraged." "Quite the contrary" commented the Oracle. "Nothing can be further from the truth; because, "love is truth and truth is love." The Oracle sensing that the woman did not understand went on to explain.

It really goes back to nature. Everyone is born with both the capacity to love and also with the capacity to hate. Which one would be expressed would be determined by how much and what kind of nurturing those genes received in the formative years. Greed, hate, intolerance, bigotry were all learned attitudes, and what was so wonderful was that with proper nurturing they could also be 'unlearned.' What happens in the home, and what happens in society, usually determines what you will become. Love a child unconditionally and he himself will learn to love unconditionally. Make your love conditional and the child will learn to love conditionally as well. Conditional love by nature limits your ability to find true happiness. It fosters insecurity, feelings of inadequacy and breeds intolerance.

If our love has conditions, for example; you must be white, or heterosexual, or thin, or Christian; then we breed intolerance, bigotry, rejection, resentment, and hatred of others and most important deep down hatred of ourselves. We must love all of God's creatures, not in spite of what they are but because of what they are. To show the importance of this concept the Oracle spoke it again. "I repeat," he said *we must learn to love all of God's creatures, not in spite of what they are but because of what they are.*" For the truth is that the richness and greatness of nature lies in its variety. We must learn to celebrate the difference. That is where the strength lies in nature, in society and that is where the strength lies in us. The strength lies in diversity. In nature the highest forms of life are the most complex. Look at an ant colony, for instance. Without, the workers, the drones, the soldiers, the engineers and the queen all working together there would be no colony. So too with mankind, we are all in this together, all creatures great and small. As a species, or for that matter as an ecosystem, we will survive or we will become extinct. But one thing is certain we will do it together. That is the truth that we must understand, we are all in this together. We live on spaceship earth. When we understand this truth, we will understand love, a love that is unconditional, a love with no hierarchy. All creatures of this planet have a right to be here, to be loved, and respected. *We must love everything not because we can get something out of it but simply because it exists.* Unconditional love is all powerful, it makes us invincible. If we make it conditional, we give all our power away to the thing we love. We give that person the power to hurt us. All that person has to do is change the conditions and we feel hurt, we may be destroyed. With love one can never say "I will love you if or I will love you when?" That makes you vulnerable. You are invincible only if it is unconditional. With love, through our respect for nature and our search for truth we will shed our shackles of distrust, our shackles of fear, intolerance, bigotry and hate. Our minds will become free. Free to look through our walls of fear. We will become all powerful as we become filled with the power of enlightenment and understanding. When we become one with truth, we become one with nature. When we become one with nature we become one with God. We become God. The change will make us beautiful. We will feel the beauty, others will feel it. It will change us. It will change them. We will love what we have become. We will be filled with love for ourselves and with that, we will have an infinite capacity to love others.

"Love, like respect, is something you must have to get."
PJ Morry 2010

The Oracle decided to give the woman a Quiz to test her understanding of his talk on love.

THE QUIZ

He said: "Why are you so rich?"
She said: "Why, what do you mean?"

He said: "Why are you rich?"
She said: "Because I have security?"

He said: "No. Try again."
She said: "Because I have integrity."

He said: "No. Try Again."
She said: "Because I have my children."
He said: "No. Try again."

She said: "Please don't tell me, because someone loves me?"

He said: "Definitely not that, for love can be taken away. No. Try again. But it is about love."

She thought and thought and thought but after about ten minutes said. "You will have to tell me."
He said: "No you already know the answer. You just have to figure it out. Tomorrow I will ask you again."

The next day:
He said: "Why are you so rich?"
She said: "Because I have love inside me?"

He said: "Yes. But what can make you even richer?"
She said: "Surely, it must be the amount of love I have inside me."

He said: "No try again. You can be filled to the top with love and overflowing. But still you can be richer"
"What will make you even richer?"
She said: "I don't know."
He said:

"Being filled with love can make you rich,
But not in every way.
The only way, you can increase your love,
Is to give your love away"

WHAT IS TRUTH?

The lesson on love was not lost on the woman. All the love she had experienced in her life to date had been conditional and she had been deeply hurt by her experiences. She resolved to be more accepting and tolerant of the failings of other and hoped that she at some point could learn to love unconditionally.

Gale was still slightly confused. She had been told many negative things about herself by her abusive husband. She had trouble distinguishing between truth and fiction. She knew that love and truth were intimately linked and that you could not have one without the other. She asked the Oracle "Is truth absolute, or can there be degrees of truth, for is it not so that you are either telling the truth or you are not. Can there be an in between? She understood that there can be varying degrees of love. Can there also be varying degrees of truth? Is there such a thing as a white lie? Can telling a lie ever be an expression of love?"

The Oracle could not help but laugh with joy, because he saw the spark of enlightenment was already growing into an ember in the woman's heart. *He* was pleased that the woman was moving into the next level of enlightenment. She was moving into the category of *"knowing she didn't know."* She was starting to think outside the box. She was starting to ask the right questions. She was starting to shed the shackles of conformity. Her growth would make her love herself, and in so doing would make her capable of loving others.

The Oracle became very pensive. It was a few moments before he answered. He postulated. "What truth is," is perhaps the greatest mystery of all. I myself am still searching for it. I have been searching for it my entire life, and still have not found it. We are born with the capacity to love, but truth is different. We are born into Ignorance and we must discover truth for ourselves. Love is an action that comes from within and can only grow when given away. Truth is a reality that is all around us. We can only find truth by looking outward, and we can only make sense of it by looking inward. There, nurtured by our love, truth will have meaning. We can only learn truth through knowledge and the journey to truth is long and the path is fraught with hazards. A child is born with an infinite capacity to love, and limited knowledge. But the journey to truth starts with limited knowledge and more knowledge can only be acquired with time. So our concept of truth will change as we grow in knowledge. As we grow in knowledge, we grow in understanding. As we grow in understanding we grow in truth. We will never know absolute truth until we have absolute knowledge. Consequently the search for absolute truth is a life long journey and will only be acquired when we become one with the cycle of awareness, and that will only be achieved when we become pure energy at our death.

River of Lies

A lie is like a river, it eats your soul away.
It wears and tears and undermines foundations made of clay.
It starts out as a trickle, innocent and yet,
You add to it, bit by bit, and soon you will regret.

The trickle becomes a rivulet, the rivulet then a stream,
And soon you lie so easily, with astonishing routine.
As water wicks its way into, every crack and seam,
So too the lie invades, pervades every fiber of you being.

And soon your carried everywhere by the river of lies you tell.
Your walls of clay and sand erode until you're just a shell.
The price you pay for all your lies is no identity.
You look into the mirror and no reflection see.

Where is the joy, the peace, the love? No moment in the sun?
Nowhere to hide, from the pain inside, from what you have become.
You realize your memory lies, like footprints on sandy shore.
A shallow grave, a single wave, and then you are no more.

The young woman was filled with the spirit of enlightenment. Renewed and invigorated with her new found understanding she set off on her journey looking for truth. She knew that as she discovered truth, she would discover love.

Chapter XVI

CONSEQUENCES

I shot an arrow into the air. It fell to earth I knew not where.
Henry Wadsworth Longfellow

The Oracle was learning a lot on his trip to Earth. He decided to visit a library and do some reading. He picked up a newspaper. He went to the people section. He read the following story titled consequences. It went as follows.

THE DRIVE BY

This morning I had an interview with John Smith who was released from prison today. He is now 32 years old and had been in prison for the last 15 years. I asked him, what was the first thing he wished to do, now that he was free. He replied to me that he never really would be free, but that he had a very busy day planned. He had to do three things. The first thing he wanted to do was to visit an old friend who had been the minister at his church and was now retired.

The minister had buried his brother and his sister. John never got to go to their burial because he was in prison at that time. He was however permitted to see a video of the proceedings. The minister had presided over that service and had spoken some words about forgiveness that really resonated with him. In fact if not for those words he would have been dead by now because those words were especially applicable to him. John now wished to visit with him, so he might share with the minister the impact that the minister's simple sermon had had on him. The second thing that John had to do was visit his brother and his sisters grave and ask for their forgiveness. The third thing he wished to do was to try and find his mother and father who were now separated.

"John's story is rather tragic" wrote the reporter. It goes as follows. "John was just 17 years old when he was sentenced to prison for life *with* the possibility of parole. He had been a model prisoner. He had done all his rehabilitation courses and had been studying law, ethics and psychology. He finally progressed to religious studies and he himself now wanted to become a minister. After 15 years he was released on parole for good behavior and was now free".

John had been convicted of murder. As a young boy of fourteen he had joined a street gang in a rough neighborhood of Los Angeles, the city of angels. He had mistakenly thought that he could end the beatings and intimidations that he received daily from other kids in the neighborhood if he was part of a gang. The city had been divided up into zones. Different gangs controlled different zones and each zone had a different color. His zone was the Reds. Every member of his gang had to wear the color red. If a rival gang member wandered into the wrong zone or was seen wearing the wrong colors in the wrong zone, he was killed! That killing then had to be avenged so there was a constant cycle of violence. Once in a gang you could not get out, you were in it for life. The currency of each zone was drugs. It was a wild and dangerous place to grow up.

He was a fat kid and was constantly being bullied and beaten up at school and on the street. He was called "fatty", and "faggot", and "sissy" and hated everyone. He thought that if he joined a gang, things would change. They did change, but for the worse. At first they got him to do little things. Things like drink alcohol and smoke pot. Then he had to be a "mule"; a term used for kids that were carrying drugs from one point to another. He would have to accompany the gangs in a car when they were doing robberies and such. At first he was a lookout, finally the moment of truth came. If he was to become a full gang member he had to be trusted. He had to be initiated. His initiation was particularly brutal. He had to do a drive by shooting.

One of the kids in his neighborhood who was not a gang member was seen selling drugs. The plan was to ambush him outside his house. They would drive by, jump out of the car, shoot him then jump back in the car again and speed away. The genius in the plan they thought was that they would dress in another gangs colors and blame it on them. The police would then be looking for members of the Blue gang and not the Reds. They would be safe. He, John Smith, would be the shooter.

Things did not go well. John was very nervous. He fired off three shoots. All three missed. They sped off. John returned home and went straight to his room. He fell asleep, and was awakened up by his father at about 11:30 at night. His father was worried. John's younger sister *Chance* age twelve had not come home. He, his brother Leroy, his father and his mother were to go looking for her. They searched for hours and could not find her. While his mother and father went to the police to report her missing, he and his brother decided to look again in a place they had previously overlooked. While walking to that site they heard the screech of brakes. As they turned to investigate, shots rang out. They dove for cover, and the car sped away. John wasn't hit. His brother Leroy was dead.

The next day John was arrested for murder. Apparently the shots that he had fired at the young man, had missed, but they had not missed everyone. The shots had gone through a window that was behind the intended target and killed a young girl. He was to realize later that the girl he accidentally shot was none other than his own sister.

To make matters worse the intended victim had a brother who was a member of a rival gang. Someone had taken a video of the shooting on a cell phone. The car they were driving and its occupants were soon identified by the rival gang. In an attempt to kill him the rival gang had shot his brother Leroy by mistake.

John had to now live with the fact that his actions had resulted in the death of his only brother and sister. Things continued to get worse.

John's father spent everything he owned on legal bills trying to keep him out of prison. His father went bankrupt. The parents blamed each other for the death of their children. If only her father had driven *Chance* to the school dance instead of letting her walk. She did not tell him that she was stopping off on the way at a friend's house. If he had driven her, both of her children would be alive today. She could not forgive him. They divorced.

John had spent the afternoon at the graveside of his brother and sister. He had cried so hard he had no more tears. He had begged their forgiveness. His next step and most important one was to try and find his mother and father. They had not spoken to him in ten years. Would they forgive him? Could they forgive him? Could he ever forgive himself? Would he ever be really free?

The Oracle thought about all the negative unintended and unpredictable consequences of the young man's actions, and wondered if little things can have positive consequences as well. He continued to read and came across the following story.

THE VALENTINE

It was Valentine's Day. It was time for all the boys and girls in the class to exchange Cards. Penny Lane age nine had attended a Girl Guide meeting the night before. The Guide leader had told all the little children a story about the value of giving your love away. She said that someday, in some way, it would come back to you and would keep on coming back to you in many different ways. She said that all you had to do is give it away and it would make you happy. She said that the more you gave your love away the happier you would become. "Tomorrow," Penny had thought, "I will try it out and see if it works".

Sitting in her class was a new boy she did not know. He never spoke to anyone, never asked questions, never smiled. His mind was always somewhere else. He was failing all his tests. He was shy and had no friends, but Penny heard her friends say that he was called *Nic*. Apparently every time he had been wronged by someone he would put one/half of an x on his belt and when he avenged that wrong he would cross that line with another line making it an X. This led to his gang giving him the name of

Nic. She wondered what was wrong. Why was Nic so mad at the world? He was only eleven years old. She wondered why he was there at all, since he never participated in anything. She decided to give her love away. She was going to give that sad lonely boy a Valentine and hoped it would make him smile. She had no idea how significant her valentine would be. She did not know that Nic was carrying a gun.

That morning, before he left for school, Nic was rummaging through a closet in an unused bedroom. He was looking for a joint of marijuana an older boy had given him the day before on the playground. He had hid it in the unused bedroom until he could get a chance to smoke it (He had planned to do so when his mom and dad were out partying Saturday night). He wanted to make sure it was still there. He found it, and hid it away again. He couldn't wait to try it. Perhaps it would make him feel better. Just as he was leaving, he got a glimpse of something shiny. It was a handgun and it was loaded. Nic stuffed the gun in his pants and hurried out of the house. He had to have a good place to hide it he may need it someday. Perhaps he would use it on himself. Perhaps he would shoot his parents. Perhaps he would kill all his classmates. Anyone who had called him names. He was not just angry. He was angry at everyone. He was angry at himself. He hated his father. He hated his mother. He hated himself.

His father an alcoholic was a big abusive aggressive bastard that beat him and his mother regularly. He had put his mom in hospital several times. He raped her repeatedly. Every night in his room Nic could hear her screaming "Please don't please don't". He even raped his 12 year sister and to make matters worse his mother knew about it and she did nothing. He knew that his mother was aware of the assault, because his sister informed him, many months ago, that she had told her mother all about it. Despite being told all the details, his mother chose not to act and the assaults by his father, her husband, on his sister continued. He hated his mother for her inaction. She was a coward. She was supposed to protect them and she did nothing. Didn't she care? She saw how he raped his sister, how he bullied him. His mother was weak and he despised her for her weakness. He despised himself because he was weak to. But that was soon to end. He was fighting back. He had a gun.

Sitting at his desk, with the gun in his pants, he felt empowered. He knew things had to change; this could not go on any longer. He had to protect his sister; he had to be a man. He was going to kill his father and then himself. Perhaps he would start in school. First he would kill those that had bullied him and then before the police could catch him rush home only minutes away where he would kill his parents and then before any chance of capture or humiliation finally kill himself. At lunch break he would kill Jake Tompkins, and Barry Walsh and his whole bunch of wannabes and then run home before anyone could figure out who did it. He looked at the clock; it was 11:30. Thirty minutes to go. Everybody was getting Valentines. Some kids got 10 or more. He did not get any. He hated them all. This would be in all the papers. People would know all about his pain. A new Valentine's Day Massacre just like Al Capone. It was 11:45. Fifteen minute to go. He murmured to himself; "That Jake Tompkins got 12 valentines the lousy bastard. He is definitely the first to go". Suddenly, he felt a hand on his shoulder. It was Penny Lane. She smiled at him, gave him a Valentine and a hug, blushed and returned to her seat without saying a word. He had to fight back the tears. He could not believe it somebody actually cared about him. He took his hand off the gun in his pocket.

That afternoon while walking home from school, he heard what sounded like a gunshot. A car tire had blown out and now a car was careening wildly. It flipped over the side of the bridge and landed upside down into a slow running stream. He ran down to the sinking car. He was a good swimmer. He swam to the car just in time to see it disappear under water. There was a woman trapped inside. Fortunately the water was only eight feet deep. The car settled to the bottom. He dove underwater and saw the woman banging on the glass. She could not get the window or door open. She was getting more frantic by the second. The car was filling up with water. Nic tried and tried but could not get the door open. His lungs were bursting. Soon she would be dead. He felt the gun in his pocket. He realized he could save her. He took the gun out of his pocket and started pounding on the glass with the butt of the gun. The glass would not break. In desperation he pulled the trigger. The concussion deafened him and made him dizzy. He became disorientated, and did not know which way was up. He was going to drown. Suddenly a hand grabbed him by the shoulder and pulled him to the surface. It was the woman. She had escaped through the back window that he had blown out with the gun.

When the police arrived and heard the boy's story they proceeded to his parent's house where they arrested his father for sexual abuse, assault and rape. The next day he found out that the woman he had saved was someone very special, she was Penny Lanes mother.

Consequences

I made a choice the other day, a tiny choice to see
I did not think that much of it, and so I set it free.
I never thought it mattered. It really was so small.
I did not think that it would have a consequence at all.

The wind it took a hold of it and blew it far and wide.
And soon I saw it disappear no longer by my side.
I forgot that I had done it, and went on with life's routine.
The tiny choice that I had made had vanished from the scene.

Like the wind through an abandoned house, my choice went everywhere.
It penetrated every crack that would admit the air.
It went up and down and all around and then came back again.
It covered me from head to toe like shirt in freezing rain.

It chilled me so I nearly died, it really frightened me.
The choice was now a consequence that nearly ended me.
Beware of choices that we make, they never are that small.
Especially the tiny ones; the ones we can't recall.

Freedom

I had a desire the other day, from deep inside of me
I could not contain it; it overflowed, and burst outside of me
If spread like magic through the air, infecting all who see
It became a fire, my deep desire, my desire to be free.

*"We are what we repeatedly do. Excellence, then,
is not an act, but a habit."*
Aristotle

Chapter XVII

"VOICES OF THE UNHEARD"

The Oracle was having a very illuminating trip around the planet Earth. He had seen how the money masters and the Power Seekers had used people's fears, ignorance, and insecurities as weapons against them. They had fueled the "us versus them" mentality to create borders and walls of indifference and hate. He had seen how nations had squandered all their resources on weapons of war and destruction leaving them impoverished and enslaved. He decided to visit one of their houses of worship to see how the spirituality of the people was expressed. He was hoping to witness expressions of love and acceptance and hear voices of tolerance and enlightenment. When he flew over one of these places of worship he was struck by a wave of shame and revulsion that seemed to emanate from one member of the congregation who was named Jacob. He decided to listen to Jake's tormented thoughts.

"What am I doing here? I feel like a hypocrite! I feel like screaming out "Get out, get out, all of you! For you are all part of the problem. We are all hypocrites." He started reminiscing.

He had three lovely children, had a loving wife who was very spiritual. His wife, who was a devout believer, sang in the church Choir. She was a rock of goodness and had always been Jake's compass; she had encouraged him to go to church. He had stopped going to church, many years ago, and it was a problem in their relationship. His wife recognized that church offered people an opportunity for reflection. In church, people could strengthen their sense of community. They could hear words of wisdom, love, forgiveness. He and his wife had had discussed the problems that had bothered him many times. Sometimes they argued. Now both of them frustrated seldom discussed the problems anymore.

Finally after many years of ignoring this significant rift in an otherwise very healthy relationship filled with mutual love and respect, Jake decided to go back to church. He returned because his wife, always a wise person and deeply moral, had said something that resonated with him so much, that he decided to become an active participant of the congregation. She had told him that "If you wanted to fix the problems you can't do it from the outside. You must do it from the inside." So he decided to go back to church. He had been driven away by the soul destroying; gut wrenching issue of child sexual abuse among the clergy. When his own child was only six, he had entertained the idea of his dearly beloved son becoming an altar boy. His parish priest a frequent guest in their house had become infamous as an abuser of children and had gone to jail. The stories Jake had heard made him sick. He felt both lucky and betrayed. Lucky because his son had narrowly missed being the victim of the most evil man he had ever known. If there was an antichrist he was it. The priest had been a pillar of the community, a man of incredible good standing. His sermons were always insightful and inspirational. For the first time in his life Jake had enjoyed going to church. He actually looked forward to the sermons and felt inspired. Now he felt betrayed because the priest was actually Lucifer in disguise. Everything he said were just words. He was a fraud. He was a pedophile with possibly hundreds of victims, and one of them could have been his own son had he become an altar boy.

Shortly after the initial revelations about his Parish Priest, Jake was invited to join a discussion panel on National television. The topic was on "Child sexual abuse". During the discussion Jake warned the audience about the dangers to young boys, who were becoming sexually aware, of going to confession. Confession was a practice among Catholics where parishioners were encouraged to talk about their sins, of all natures, to a priest in a dark enclosed cubical called the confessional. The only thing between the priest and the confessor was a thin curtain. Most of the confessors could be recognized by their voice and also possibly seen. At that time masturbation was considered a sin in the Catholic Church and still is. Jake considered it a huge risk for young boys to talk about anything sexual to such a powerful figure as a priest, a person who could be a sexual predator. These young impressionable boys were encouraged by their church to confess their transgressions and to ask for penance and absolution. Jake by discussing his concerns on National Television caused an uproar amongst the clergy who were still in denial about the risks involved in confession, but despite pressure to recant, he did not back down. He felt he had done something positive. Time passed and the issue disappeared from public consciousness and in most cases individual as well. The boys had been forgotten, people moved on.

All seemed well for several years, but in reality not much had changed. The initial shock of the revelation of sexual abuse of young boys by priests' had worn off. Over the years there had been a steady stream of revelations, church after church, city after city, country after country, organization after organization. The world was full of it and people no longer seemed to care and it became business as usual. Few of the perpetrators got significant punishments and the victims got little help with their shattered lives.

Jake was aroused from his reminiscence by his fellow parishioners singing a hymn. He drifted off again. He was recalling an encounter he had with a young man in Vancouver a few years earlier. This man was homeless and sleeping on a park bench. The homeless man was begging for money. He had become addicted to heroin and cocaine. He spoke with an accent that Jake immediately recognized. Like himself the homeless man was from Newfoundland. Knowing that the homeless man would probably spend the money on drugs Jake offered to buy him a coffee and a hot breakfast. He accepted. On their way to the coffee house they talked.

The poor wretch had grown up in Mount Cashel Orphanage in St. John's Newfoundland. There he had been sexually abused for years by several of the "Irish Christian Brothers," the custodians of the orphanage. Several times he had confided his troubles to a higher authority and on one occasion even ran away and told his story to a police officer. On every occasion he had been brought back to his abuser and invariably he was beaten. On one occasion he was beaten so badly he had to be hospitalized. Finally one day at the age of fifteen he ran away never to return. He had to turn to prostitution to survive and now here he was homeless in Vancouver. He was thirty five years of age, addicted to heroin and cocaine, and HIV positive. To make matters worse every day he would see the person that victimized him. The park bench which was his home overlooked a set of duplex apartments connected to a religious institution. His abuser after serving five years in prison for his offences was living there and working there. Every day the victim would see his nemesis drive around in his Cadillac car: he was living in luxury, while he himself was living in hell. He felt he was being abused again, every day. He broke down crying. Jake felt inadequate and helpless. He paid for the meal and left $20.00 with the waitress for another meal for the man. He left. That memory would never leave him. The thousands of child abuse victims now had a face, a face that he would never forget.

Still in church, Jake was again jerked back to reality by the prayers of the congregation. For years he had suppressed his feelings of anger and disgust for the child abusers that dwelt within the confines of the clergy. These feelings were aroused yet again during his encounter with the homeless man. However, today his wounds were reopened by new allegations of even greater evil. He could not get it out of his mind. The allegations were worse than ever before. He felt like an absolute fool. Fool me once shame on you, fool me twice shame on me. He felt like running out of the church.

He had watched a BBC Documentary on the news yesterday titled *Sex and the Vatican* and regretted going to church today. It was a mistake. He vowed never to come back again. He felt like bolting out the door. He felt ashamed to be there. He did not belong there. He felt like a hypocrite.

The day before the BBC had aired on television another documentary on child sexual abuse that again had shaken him to the core. It had been alleged that the newly elected Pope of The Roman Catholic Church had for years been in charge of a secret program designed to cover up cases where priests were accused of sexual abuse against young boys. Witness after witness had come forward on camera and accused the newly elected Pope of having been complicit in covering up sexual abuse of young boys by the clergy. Apparently before being elected, the newly elected Pope had been appointed by the Vatican to oversee all allegations of sexual abuse by the clergy against young boys. It was alleged that the official policy was to deny, delay and frustrate. It was alleged that the Pope Elects job before becoming Pope was not to investigate allegations of abuse, with the goal of getting at the truth and seeking justice, but was to cover-up whenever possible. Apparently he had done this job for years and had done it well. Now he was the Pope. It was alleged that his job was to move the accused priests to different parishes where they continued to abuse new kids. Supposedly complaints languished on the soon to be Popes' desk for years gathering dust. Often there was intimidation. Nothing had changed and nothing was changing. Jake was outraged. His mind and soul screamed *"WHO WAS LOOKING OUT FOR THE BOYS AND THEIR FAMILIES?* This man was now our spiritual leader, our Pope, and God's representative on Earth. This was the man we were supposed to look to for guidance and wisdom. Our teachings told us that he the Pope was infallible.

The newly elected Pope just ignored the accusations and the accusers, as did everyone else. There was no formal police investigation, no charges laid. There was no trial, nothing. No formal denial was made. Not any invitation by the Vatican for the police to come and investigate. If there was any investigation, Jake was not aware of it. It was business as usual. Everything was swept under the rug. There were no denials, no affirmations, no resignations, no day in court. These accusers and their allegations were swept under the rug. It is as if they did not exist, as if they never existed. Where was the public outcry? His silence made him guilty. "What am I doing here? Shouldn't I be screaming out my sense of outrage"? By being silent, he had become part of the problem. He had become a hypocrite, surrounded by a sea of hypocrites.

Jake felt nauseated. He felt ashamed for not having the courage to cry out in church. This Pope was supposed to be a man of God, the spiritual leader of millions. How could he do what he did and still be a Pope? Where was the outcry? Who was speaking out for these victims?

The Oracle could see that the parishioner felt like he was in Nazi Germany, standing up watching a helpless Jew being bullied and beaten, and he was doing nothing. Jake remembered a quote that he had once proudly displayed on his webpage: "Evil triumphs when good men do nothing". He felt like screaming out in the church for all to here, "The Pope should resign! He should be in jail!" He did not. He remained silent. He felt ashamed. He felt like a coward. No one was standing up for these boys? He wasn't. He was just as bad as those that he was accusing. He felt dirty. By not speaking out, he had become part of the problem. He became nauseated and nearly vomited. He did not speak out. He left the church feeling ashamed.

Chapter XVIII

AGEING

The ageing woman was contemplating her life. Now sixty she was re- evaluating everything. Life was now on the fast track as she was contemplating the ravages of cancer, how the disease would change all her plans and make her take stock of her relationships and the meaning of life itself.

> *"Young lovers seek perfection. Old lovers learn the art of sewing threads together and see beauty in a multiplicity of patches."*
> —From: How to Make an American Quilt

"Thoughts of an Ageing Man"

Gone are the dreams of youth, that sense of invincibility, the unawareness of time, the nights of falling asleep with mind soaring on dreams of tomorrow! Now nights are sleepless, as the reality of days shortened and dreams dashed fill my mind. Now I struggle with feelings of folly for reckless choices made when there was no sense of lack of time.

Procrastination and dreams of destination disguise the passage of youth. Ruthless routine flattens perception, blending past, present, and future into one. The future arrives like an airplane out of nowhere, having seen nothing between here and there. Suddenly we are old, bewildered by the transformation.

Reformation now must be the priority, as precious dreams now unrealistic vanish. Rusted relationships, ruined by neglect, must now be rescued.

Deeds, not dreams, here not there, must now resuscitate a dulled brain that has long since forgotten that relationships hold the meaning of life.

The transformation if successful, entails being content with what I have, letting go of ever increasingly distant dreams, returning to the familiar shores of youth, and the love of family and friends. There bathed by oceans mists, and the thunder of breaking waves I will spend the rest of my days in simpler times until the soils of home reclaim my soul.

"More Thoughts of an Ageing Man"

Soon I will be no more, my journey ended. It has been brief, and I wonder how I shall spend the rest of it. Like the rose that is fading, past its glory. Faded now, does my presence, devoid of color, vigor, scent, cease to have meaning? How do I bring joy to the room that was my life now that I am spent? The eyes that held my beauty, the nose that felt my presence will soon seek new pleasures, for life goes on. My Fading remains will soon have to find new joy in nurturing the souls of new creatures of the earth that will welcome my presence, and give me new meaning.

Chapter XIX

"THE MEANING OF LIFE"

The Oracle was suddenly overwhelmed by a profound sense of loneliness and pain. It seemed to come from a middle-aged women standing transfixed in a doorway, unsure of whether or not she should go, dreading the first step of a brief yet painfully long journey to the hospital. What would she say? *What could she say?* What if her sister was silent? Her beloved sister had cancer, and the recent news was far from good. Incurable! The word echoed in her mind. As a nurse she had seen death many times, yet she felt scared, inadequate, and abandoned? She had long since stopped practicing nursing and had herself become a patient. She was a simple person, kind and compassionate. She was born to be a caregiver; it came naturally, and in her day she had been very good at it. Her gifts of a kind heart and gentle touch had served her well over the years, but now she felt utterly helpless. She had three good children, a supportive husband to guide her, yet she had lost her way. There were many times when she could hardly look in the mirror. Although an attractive woman on the outside, Elaine did not like what she saw on the inside. She hated mirrors. Arthritis had filled her life with pain; it consumed her mind, body and soul, inescapable and relentless. She had become addicted to Oxycontin. The irony was so thick she could choke on it; a healer destroyed by her own hand. She hated how it had enslaved her free spirit and robbed her of the gift of giving joy, joy which she no longer possessed. She was from a large family but there was no closeness only distance between them. Relationships were fractured and the splinters pierced her heart. As a caregiver Elaine longed to heal. Care giving was what she did best, and now that her sister was ill she was unsure of what to do. Was it her fault? Her circle of friends had shrunk to a pin. She hardly went out anymore. The isolation made her angry, made her depressed. She loved her sister dearly and the thought of losing her was unbearably and frightening; not only because she was losing a loved one, but because it reminded her of her own mortality, of her own failure. She was running out of time. What was the meaning of it all? Why did this happen to my beautiful sister? Why her? Why me? Why not me? Fear gripped her. Feeling sad and inadequate she went to the hospital.

The visit to the hospital had gone badly, worse than expected. Silences were long, deafening. Things that needed to be said were not yet said. Walls of pain and denial were left intact, impenetrable! Yet she had done it. She had gone. Amongst all the despair and desperation had come a moment of inspiration. Elaine would take her sister to the ocean. They would go to Ferryland.

Ferryland

On The Beaches In Ferryland

Oh the days are getting shorter, and the waves keep rolling in
The chill is in the ocean breeze, as it whisks around my chin

The moonbeams sparkle on the rocks, wet with the snowy foam.
The stars they sparkle in the sky, on this land that I call home.

My heart can't help but be at peace, when I sit upon this rock.
The oceans roar, the tidal bore, the magic of this spot.

The shipwreck lies there silent. It's days of roaming done.
I cannot help but know that I will be another one.

For I've roamed this wide world over. I've searched it far and wide.
The only peace that I can find is by the shipwreck's side.

It looks so peaceful lying there. Its soul has been released.
The lighthouse light it beckons there, to come and find your peace.

The thunder, crashing, of the waves, my God has brought me near.
In quiet peaceful solitude I rest and know no fear.

For the ocean is both war and peace. It is both life and death.
It gives me inspiration. It brings me home to rest.

I see this shipwreck lying there, while ships are sailing past.
The restless seagulls overhead. The spirit of my past.

For now I gladly settle down, beside my shipwreck friend.
The quiet beauty of this place will be my journeys' end.

Peter Paula Pat Gaze

Ghost of the Torhamvan

Renewed by her experience at the beach with her dying sister, Elaine contemplated with healing heart the meaning of life. The impending death of her sister had reminded her of life's importance, sanctity, beauty. She would maximize the time she had remaining with her sister and counted each and every day with her sister not as one day less to live, but as one more day to love and to nurture. Her sister's illness had given her an opportunity to help, to nurture and to love . . . She recalled some words that were said to her by her doctor when, she had sought his council only a few days earlier. "Life is not measured by the number of breaths you take, but by the number of moments that take your breath away." (*Hilary Cooper*) She was no longer dreading the impending loss of her sister but was treasuring the opportunity given to her to bring new meaning into her own life and to that of her sister. In a strange way her loneliness had been supplanted by contentment. She looks at all life differently now. Time had no meaning. It was not to be feared. The iceberg she had seen with her sister in Ferryland had been around for thousands of years and in a few weeks would be gone, not dead but transformed. Death was not an end, but a transformation.

Man on Iceberg Ferryland July 2012

Ode To An Iceberg

Oh aged wonder of young earth's pole,
Majestic Mountain of ice so pure,
You chill the water, air, and soul,
With Cathedral Spires to heaven soar.

With colour white and blue and green,
You Grace this bleak and barren scene.
You gouge the earth with trenches deep,
Yet barely above the surface peep.

Huge mass of ice to heaven rise,
With towers reaching to the skies.
Yet nine-tenths below the surface hide
To ambush those that surface ride.

Ten thousand years you've prowled since birth,
Powdered mountains to fertile earth,
Nourished rivers, valleys, plains,
With captured water from winter's rains.

Like God's plough you gouge the soil,
While around you, seething waters boil.
Renewing life to fish and sea.
God's great gift to you and me.

Great berg, Oh nature's wonder beast,
You are God's messenger and God's priest.
Remind vain man of where we stand,
A blink in time, a grain of sand.

Why am I Here

Who will remember me when I am gone?
Will there be tears, reminiscence, song?
What is the meaning of my brief light?
Was I a candle seen in the night?
Or was I a wind invisible to sight?
My presence not felt or remembered.

Was I a rain drop in the river of life,
A grain of sand on the ocean floor,
A brilliant star that shone in the night,
Or dust in the wind, remembered no more?

Why am I here?
From whence did I come?
Am I the cold of the night?
Or the warmth of the sun?
The meaning of life, be I a rock or a tree,
Why am I here? What purpose in me?

What meaning in time, as millennia do pass?
When great mountain peaks, like ice in a glass,
Melt into the sea in a fraction of time,
Leaving no trace of their existence behind!

Why am I here, in this instant in time?
Where is the meaning, the reason, the rhyme?
There is only one answer, one reason to be.
Only one truth, that gives meaning to me.

From the depths of the ocean, to the stars up above.
All I can do—IS LOVE.

Chapter XX

"DEATH AND DYING"

For the first time in the history of Perpetua a seeker had died. Shockwaves rippled across the land with the news. Fear gripped all the seekers everywhere in all the villages. Why did this happen, what does it mean? What do we do now? In the beginning when Perpetua was perfect there was no stress and no time and no aging. The Power Seekers by controlling access to the sources of knowledge had robbed the seekers of their freedom to think outside the box. The search for truth and knowledge had brought with it peace and tranquility and had been the life force of the seekers. Now it was replaced by the forces of conformity, self-righteousness, bigotry, intolerance, and greed. Instead of being filled with the joy of discovery as in a new born child the seekers were filled with the fear of the unknown. Lives were filled with stress and the spirits of the seekers weighed down by their load of ignorance were no longer able to soar, no longer able to become one with nature, no longer able to become pure energy, as it was in the beginning when freedom, truth and knowledge ruled the land.

Unable to tap into the wisdom of the cosmic consciousness the seekers had lost their way. No longer able to renew their spirits with the energy that come from seeking the truth they had become old. The stress of starving their spirits of new found knowledge had caused their bodies to age and their minds to wither and death had finally come to Perpetua. No one understood what was happening and all were fearful. Not knowing the true meaning of life the seekers were confused and fearful of death, fearful of what comes after, if anything. Some of the Power Seekers seized on these fears and used them to gain more power.

They organized themselves into churches, synagogues, temples, mosques and charged the people money to show them the way back to Paradise. They organized themselves into religions and each said the other was wrong. Wars were fought and the truth was never found. Within these organizations there were some individual seekers that thought they had the right message, but usually intolerance and self-righteousness prevented them from truly understanding the message of love they were preaching, for their love was conditional. Because their love was conditional and everyone disagreed on what the conditions were, they were never able to really understand the true meaning of love. And because everyone had a different meaning for truth they were never able the get at the real meaning of truth. As a result, few were able to soar and tap into the cosmic consciousness and death became a permanent feature in Perpetua.

Chapter XXI

SHADES OF GREY

This time the Oracle's visit to Earth had been extremely interesting. On his many journeys around the planet, he had seen much. He had seen war, hate, self-hate, love, and something which she had not yet seen on his own planet of Perpetua something called death. In his desire to find out more about this the Oracle with his passenger Bill decided to drop in on situations where death was either occurring or was being discussed. He had a lot to learn and the journey would be very illuminating.

He found an aging physician, affectionately known to his friends as PJ, who was reviewing a journal of his memoires that he had kept over the years. PJ was thinking about some of the challenging situations he had to face over the 35 years of practice. He had practiced in several countries and he had experienced a lot of memorable moments filled with ethical and moral dilemmas that had caused him much concern at the time. The Oracle found a number of these memories of profound interest and viewed each one in detail.

The Old Couple:

He viewed a scene where PJ then a young doc was talking to an old couple who had been married for over 50 years. The old man, who once weighed 250 pounds, was now barely 80. He looked tired and worn and he was obviously dying. He had been battling cancer for over two years. Had gone through surgery, chemotherapy, radiation, and now nothing further could be done and the end was near. His wife had been very supportive and she had gone through a long period of nurturing. All their lives they had been close, but this long, tragic illness had brought them even closer. They had done all that needed to be done, and said all that needed to be said. He was now ready to die and wished his pain and suffering to end. He had discussed this with his wife, and she agreed that enough was enough. They approached PJ for help in achieving their mutual goal of ending his pain.

PJ certainly appreciated the sincerity of their request; he also knew the gravity of it, for he was very aware that the community at large frowned on physicians getting involved in such activities and for the most part requests of such nature were denied. PJ found himself trapped in a dilemma. On the one hand, he had grown to respect and appreciate the deep love that the old couple had for each other, and he understood their request because it came from love. He felt their pain and wanted to help, but was unsure of what he could do given the gravity and the complexity of the situation. After long conversation with the couple the young physician advised them that he would think about it and left.

A Lesson for a Student

PJ had encountered this situation several times before in his young career. Never, ever before had the decision been a difficult as it was today. He remembered when as an intern doing his pediatric rotation in medical school, he had to face a decision similar to this one. He had been working on call in the hospital when he got a page to go to the pediatric floor where a young 12-year-old boy was gravely ill. The young boy had developed pneumonia; however it was an unusual situation. The young boy had been in hospital since the age of two, when he had developed meningitis which had ravaged his brain and left him unable to speak, unable to walk, unable to move and completely unaware of his surroundings. He was a vegetable. Such an ugly word, and yet nothing else seemed to fit.

The child had been kept alive for 10 years with the feeding tube in the stomach and every day nurses turned him, bathed him, cleaned him, and cared for his every need. Despite the exemplary level of care the boy had developed contractures in his arms and legs and was permanently fixed in the fetal position. He lay there like a block of wood and was turned regularly to avoid bed sores which fortunately he never developed. His parents and all relatives had long since stopped visiting him. The last time he had a visitor was seven years prior. PJ having examined the patient determined that he had had pneumonia. Now he was unsure of what to do. Should he treat it, or should he not treat it? What was the point of treating him, since he was never going to get better? The boy was not aware that he was in the world. No one except the nurses cared. What should he do then? The cruel reality was that there were not enough resources to provide all the medical care that was needed to all the people. Perhaps the money spent on this young child could be better spent on someone who may need dialysis or some other major treatment? Withdrawing treatment already started was actually doing something and definitely would require consultation, but was not treating, not doing anything, not initiating treatment the same? This was indeed a moral dilemma, not sure of what to do PJ consulted a pediatrician to get his opinion.

When the situation was explained to the pediatrician the pediatrician's answer was immediate and unequivocal." Of course you treat." PJ sensing the sureness in the reply of the pediatrician asked the question "but why did you say *of course you have to treat*?" The pediatricians reply was quite clear and understandable and PJ ordered penicillin and the child survived. The pediatrician had left a lasting impression on the young physician. For years the nurses had cared for that child, had fed him, had bathed him, and had nurtured him. How would they feel about the value of their work if we were to just simply let him die? It was a good lesson about the value of human life and the gravity of any decision that impacts it. We all get value out of helping the sick, and all life no matter how configured is to be treasured. This was the message that PJ took away from that experience. He found himself asking himself this question. "We as caregivers must provide care for those who through mental incompetence cannot care for themselves; but what about those of sound mind? What are their rights? Does a terminally ill patient of sound mind have the right to choose how and when he or she dies"?

The decision regarding the old man was not a simple One. The old man and his wife were of sound mind, and her thinking was clear. Did they not have the right to determine their own destiny? PJ realized he needed to deliberate some more.

I'M FINE THANK YOU

While deliberating whether or not people are capable of making decisions regards their own death, PJ remembered an experience that he had early in his career, when treating an 80-year-old man who had developed a complete heart block. The old man was showing signs of heart failure with swelling, and shortness on this breath. The old man had had tests completed that had confirmed the presence of an electrical problem in the heart, which was fixable with a pacemaker. PJ had explained to the patient, that a simple operation could correct the problem, and he assured the old man that he could live a normal life and have a normal life expectancy.

To his surprise, the patient refused the surgery. The physician decided to have a long talk with the patient to make sure that he, the patient, understood the consequences of his decision. Having done so the physician felt assured that the old man knew what he was doing. The old man had said." I have lived a long life. I have enjoyed my life. I have a great family. I would like to live another 15 or 20 years, but if I die tomorrow, I am ready. I do not want the surgery." Having convinced himself that the own man was indeed cognizant of the consequences of his decision the PJ decided not to intervene any further and let nature take its course. A week later the old man died.

That encounter with the old man taught the PJ a lot. He realized that sometimes people are ready to die and that being ready does not necessarily connote a dysfunction, or a depression. Sometimes, when you've had a full and complete life and you are happy and content, dying is not something to be feared but to be embraced as if one is going on a new journey. It is not necessarily an end but maybe a beginning. He remembered a quote that he had read during the course of his own life journey: ***"Life is not measured by the number of breaths we take, but the number of moments that take our breath away."*** *(Hilary Cooper)*

LEUKEMIA

A stark contrast to the previously discussed situation had presented itself to the young physician only a few years after graduation. He had gone to a small town to practice. One of his patients, a young boy of 10, had developed Leukemia. The young boy had undergone a couple years of chemotherapy but now had become resistant to all forms of treatment. The parents have been told that nothing more could be done for their son, so he was sent home to die.

One night around 10 o'clock, PJ got an emergency call to go to the young boy's home. The boy had started bleeding. He was bleeding out of his nose, his eyes, and his ears. His skin was covered with bruises. He was crying incessantly, short of breath, and was in pain. His eyes were filled with terror. The parents were extremely alarmed and pleaded for help. It was instantly obvious to the physician what was happening. The boy's blood was now so thin that he was bleeding to death internally and externally. The child was struggling to breathe. He was drowning in his own blood. PJ explained to the parents what was happening and they asked him how long it would take their son to die. He informed the parents that he did not know exactly but it would probably be a matter of hours rather than minutes. The physician could see in their eyes that the thought of their son suffering like that for hours was unbearable to them.

He said "I could give the child some Morphine which would help ease his pain and sedate him so he would not be terrified." He explained to them that their sons lungs were filling up with blood a shot of Morphine would most likely hasten his demise because of its effect of further depressing the child's respiration. He asked the parents if that was what they wanted him to do. Without hesitation, the parents requested that he give their boy Morphine, anything, to alleviate his suffering. Within a minute or so of giving the young boy ten mg of morphine he settled. He stopped screaming and lay peacefully in his sleep. Less than an hour later he died. Having watched a child suffer so much, the parents expressed relief at the moment of his death. Truly when things get bad enough, death can be your friend.

THE DOCTORS' DILEMMA

The Oracle on scanning the journal had noticed that the Physician PJ had not only witnessed the death of several children but had witnessed the death of one of his own children as well. In that particular case, the Oracle noted that PJ being trapped in a situation where he was the attending physician during his own child's death was a very unusual experience and was definitely worth a review. *The Oracle knew that there was the risk of being somewhat repetitive as the matter was discussed earlier from the point of view of the parent. (Refer to chapter Ten) but he decided to continue probing this point in PJ's memoires.*

PJ had to give CPR to his own child who had been found by his mother in his crib, mottled, not breathing and with no pulse. Presented with his unconscious and possibly dead son he immediately started CPR on the child but after 30 min. nothing was happening except that now the child's abdomen was bloated and his mouth was full of vomit. Alex was not responding. Thoughts were going through his father's head, horrible thoughts. What if he doesn't make it? What if he does make it? Would he be a vegetable, would he ever talk or walk? He had visions of the nightmare his life would become if his child survived. While performing CPR on his son the physician shared his concerns that Alex would not make it with his wife, who was in shock and could not believe what, was happening. He visualized years and years of going to the hospital to spend time with a child that would never speak, perhaps in a permanent coma like the child he had attended when he was a medical student. He knew that the stress of that ordeal could mean the end of his marriage. He knew that he would feel guilt when he wasn't there in the hospital with his child. He would also feel guilt when he was there because he knew visiting Alex would take away from the time he could spend with his other children. It would be a lose / lose situation. He wanted to stop CPR but he couldn't.

He continued to give CPR but the situation was getting hopeless, no it was hopeless. Dare I stop? Dare I continue? What if he does survive, will our married survive it? With years of visiting a hospital every day, while, neglecting the needs of the other children, be worth it? If I do stop will I ever be sure I didn't quit too early?

Eventually it became obvious that nothing was going to save the child. After what seemed like an eternity, compressed into forty minutes. The physician asked his wife should he stop or should he continue. Of course his wife was unable to answer she was in shock. He did not expect an answer. No mother could answer that question, But he had to tell her what he was thinking, he had to prepare her for the decision he was about to make. He was about to stop CPR. He told her he was going to stop. She did not react. She said nothing. She did nothing. He hoped she understood what was happening. He was going to stop CPR. Then there would be no doubt, his child would be dead. He looked up at her and spoke the unspeakable "I'm stopping". He stopped. He sat there with a heavy heart, in shock himself. His child was dead.

The ambulance soon arrived but it was too late. Still in shock the parents accompanied their dead son to the hospital, the mother cradled her baby boy in her arms. Nothing was said. What could be said? There simply were no words.

PJ sat their reading his journal. He knew that when considering the Old man's request, his recollection of his own feelings, thoughts, actions and consequences revolving around the death of his own son were still painfully fresh in his mind and were no doubt going to factor into the decision he would soon have to make. The two situations, which on the surface appeared very different, in essence had enough similarities to give him a better ability to empathize not only with the dying man but his surviving wife.

The Oracle had seen into the young physician's mind. He instantly knew all that he had seen and all that he had done. He still did not know what the physician would do with the request of the old man and his wife. That decision had not yet been made. The Oracle continued to probe the physician's thoughts.

CHOOSING THE TIME

Still deliberating about what to do about the old man's request, PJ remembered his own father's death. His own father had died of congestive heart failure and his death had not been easy.

His father had died only two years earlier and his recall of the last few days was crystal clear. His father, for about six months, had been suffering from congestive heart failure. He had had an aortic heart valve replaced 30 or more years earlier and had done remarkably well. Up until the age of eighty-five, he could still walk 5 to 10 miles per day and would do it religiously, however at the age of eighty-six things started to change. Although his brilliant mind was still crystal clear he was getting short of breath when he lay down and on exertion. No longer could he do his long walks and that frustrated him. Having a photographic memory and being a voracious reader, he was always engaged in one cause or another. Being a veteran of WWII he was passionately involved with the legion, the Singing Legionnaires, and too many volunteer organizations to enumerate. Suffice it to say he was a giant among men, but seemed unaware of his impact on the world which was substantial. He was not a humble man, and his intellect was intimidating.

PJ's thoughts drifted away from the circumstances of his father's death, and he fondly reminisced about an event that happened only a few months before he died. He had been at his home when his father came to visit. His father was a stoic; and so the young physician never really got to know him. His father rarely discussed his own personal life, and almost never showed his true feelings. He was a deeply private person. Despite that, PJ never doubted his father's integrity or his love. His father was honest to a fault and yet in his entire life had only once told his son that he loved him. That event occurred when his father had just come out of the OR having just had heart surgery. His father still heavily sedated, returned his sons expressions of love with his own "I love you". His father was a man who never admitted he was wrong and to make matters worse seldom was.

PJ fondly recalled a day in his kitchen, when he was discussing with his best friend some poetry he had written. His father then aged 85 walked into the kitchen and hearing the conversation did something that PJ would never forget. His father said. "PJ has always written poetry. He started when he was a boy of ten. At that age he wrote a poem to Frank Mahovalich his hockey hero and Mr. Mahovalich sent him an autographed picture". He then recited the eight verse poem in its entirety, a poem that PJ the author had long since forgotten. PJ was blown away, since he had written that poem more than fifty years previously. His father Will then went on the recite another poem that PJ had written to him for his fortieth birthday some 46 years earlier. "My God, PJ exclaimed to himself, I thought he didn't care".

His father's illness was difficult. At night Will would start to suffocate every time he lay down, so most nights he would have to sleep sitting up. He would be terrified that he was going to smother. His son had returned to his practice in British Columbia and was constantly told by the cardiologist that it was not Will's heart that was causing his shortness of breath. The cardiologist had Will admitted to the Waterford, a psychiatric hospital. The cardiologist had diagnosed a panic disorder. He was wrong. Fortunately for Will, his daughter in law had come back from BC to care for him. She was a Godsend. She was a nurturing, kind woman with an amazingly perceptive mind. She could at first glance read people like a book. She spent hours talking to Will and took him everywhere he wished to go. She cared for his every need, and got to know him better than anyone. She was able to get rid of all his demons, many of which were there from his war years and his childhood. He mellowed. She had long talks with him and broke down walls that were a lifetime in the making.

It soon became obvious to the psychiatrist that Will's shortness of breath was not due to a panic disorder. Unfortunately Wills admission to the Waterford Hospital did nothing for his heart failure and he continued to deteriorate at an alarming rate. His weight increased by over forty pounds, it was all fluid and a large portion of it was on his lungs. He was drowning. The cardiologist was still telling his son in BC that his father was doing as well as expected and no suggestion that things were in dire straits was given. His son alarmed by what his wife was telling him flew home to see for himself. His father would be dead in less than a week.

The last days spent with Will were precious and very illuminating and had great relevance in helping PJ resolve the dilemma that had been troubling him for weeks. How could he ethically help the old man end his pain and suffering.

The last few days with Will were precious. All the family was gathered around and Will had time to have a one on one chat with all of them. There were to be five precious days of meaningful relationships. For the most part there was silence. But the silence was pregnant with love and sharing. Will spoke with a gentleness and peace in his voice not often seen before. In his talk with his son PJ, three days before his death, he had extracted from him a promise that when the time came and he was ready to go his son would help him. When he was ready to let go, he would tell his son who promised that he would do all in his power to help his father achieve his wish. His father knew that his son would act on that promise since his son had taken a page from his father's own book and was a man of his word. His son was determined to be like him.

To the end, Will maintained that brilliant clarity of thought that his son had come to admire. For another day things remained stable and for hours bedside vigilance was maintained. The time was packed with many tender moments and there were moments of humor as well. Too weak for a belly laugh, Will still managed a smile. In his last moments Will gave three requests to his son. Then having finished all his business he looked his son straight in the eye and said "Get me out of here as quickly as possible" He could barely get out the words his breath was so short and there was a look of panic in his eyes as he started to smother. His son, the physician called in the attending doctor and Will was given 10 mg of Morphine. His father drifted into a temporary sleep. PJ was acutely aware that the drug would wear off in about thirty minutes and that his father would probably wake up again, something he did not want his father to do because of his promise to him. PJ had a talk with the attending doctor. He told him about his father's request and his own promise. The attending physician asked for time to discuss the situation with the specialist and would soon return.

Fifteen minutes later he came back and asked the son a question. "Is your father in pain?" The son being a doctor and acutely aware of what the attending physician was actually saying and remembering the death of the young boy with leukemia years ago, he gave an affirmative answer. "Yes my father is in a lot of Psychological Pain" The attending physician said nothing. He left the room. His father's orders for pain medication were increased to insure that his father was kept sedated andcomfortable. He never regained consciousness.

For hours and hours the family stayed with Will. His breathing became more labored and more irregular. There were times when he would stop breathing for almost a minute and start up again. The "words as quickly as possible" echoed in his sons head. He lowered the head of his father's bed knowing that such action would hasten his father's death. His wife knowing what her husband was doing looked at him disapprovingly. She said nothing and did nothing. Ten minutes later a nurse came in and seeing that the bed was too low raised it. Wills breathing improved slightly. The son never lowered it again.

They continued to watch Will breath for hours and hours. Many times they thought he was gone but he always came back. Finally after two days, exhausted PJ left the room to try and get some sleep. His wife always the nurturer fought off the exhaustion and never left Will's bedside. So it was also for his granddaughter who Will lovingly called Becwec. Like her mother she was a caring loving person who always had the ability to dig down in times of need. A few hours later Becca awakened her dad in the other room. His father was dead.

The Oracle was very interested in seeing what the young physician was going to do with his moral dilemma He decided he would observe the physician for awhile longer to see what he would do. He knew the physician had acquired a lot of experience over the years, but had he acquired wisdom? What would he decide?

Over the years PJ had learned to appreciate the fact that he had been privileged to have been a part of the most significant events in anybody's life. He had delivered many babies, been to many weddings, and witnessed many deaths. He had talked to his patients about their deepest concerns, about their biggest fears. He had been tested with many ethical dilemmas.

He had made his own share of mistakes. He had learned a lot here and there. The more he learned the more sensitive he became to the fact that the world of ethics like an onion had many layers. He realized there was still much more to be learned. He only hoped that concerning the old couple, he would be able to balance his deep sense of compassion and commitment to help them, with the first tenant of the Hippocratic oath which was" first do no harm". He continued to think deeply and soberly about what he should do.

TRISOMY XIII

He reflected on another time when he would be called on to deal with the death of a child. This child had not yet been born, but he had to inform the parents that the child would have an eighty percent chance of dying within a few days of delivery. An ultrasound showed that the child had Trisomy XIII and the physician knew that very few children would live to adulthood. The child would be born with many severe abnormalities.

Most of the abnormalities would be severe. The child would be mental and motor challenged; have microcephaly (a very small head), holoprosencephaly (failure of the forebrain to develop properly), Microphthalmia (an eye disorder), cataracts, retinal detachments, blindness, Polydactyl (extra fingers), mmeningomyelocoele (a spinal cord defect), Omphalocoele (an abdominal wall defect), low set ears, cleft pallet, abnormal genitalia, kidney defects, heart defects, and other less severe defects.

This condition is rare; deadly to the child, and obviously devastating to a family. The decision to abort it or carry it to term knowing that it will mostly either die shortly after birth or live a lifetime in an institution with very limited ability to have meaningful interactions with its environment. Abortion is never easy decision. Such was the case with this young couple. Both were wonderful, caring individuals, both were committed to each other and both were deeply religious.

The physician was deeply aware of the devastating effect that carrying a severely defective baby for months or of losing a baby during pregnancy or having the baby die shortly after birth could have on a mother and on her whole family. Having such a severely dysfunctional baby could, over time, be even more devastating. He was also aware how difficult it was to opt for an abortion when one has to live in a religious community where rightly or wrongly people make your deeply personal business their business. He had seen how public sanctions for a decision made could easily destroy a family. The couple had to decide whether to abort or not. That decision whatever it would be would surely define their relationship, and it did.

He had seen how personal guilt for a decision made could haunt for a lifetime. He realized his role was never to make a decision for a patient. His role was to guide them, to make sure that they had all the information needed to make their own decision. Never in his own career would he violate his deep respect for a patient's right to make their own choices. He knew that these issues were never black or white and always were life changing. He considered the young couple and what had happened to them when he thought about his dilemma with the old man. He would have to make a decision soon, because he would be moving thousands of miles away in only three days. He was moving back to Newfoundland.

DECISION TIME

All those years of practice, and all the difficult decisions that he had to make in the past, had barely prepared him for the one that he was about to make. This situation was a bit different. Although death was inevitable it was still probably weeks away. However the man had had enough.

He was intelligent, loving, understanding, and spiritual. He had a long and loving relationship with his wife, and had three loving children. He had enjoyed his life, said all he had to say, and was now ready to meet his maker. He was bedridden, in constant pain, and physically a shell of what he had once been. He wanted to end it. He wanted help. The simplest thing for the physician to do would be to walk away and say" I can't help you. I can't help you". He could not say the words, yet he knew that would be the easy way out. Saying those words would in his eyes also mean that he had failed his patient, and failed his patient's wife. The patient had gone through the five steps of death. 1. Denial and Isolation; 2. Anger; 3. Bargaining; 4. Depression; 5. Acceptance. He had accepted his fate. He was ready. Protocol would require that the physician send the patient to a psychiatrist. He knew that from the Sue Rodriguez Case that the more people got involved the less likely the patient would get a satisfactory outcome. The man did not want a long drawn out evaluation, he was ready now.

There was no need for a Psychiatrist. There was no need for anti depressants. The patient was not depressed, he was not confused, he was not afraid of death. He welcomed death. The physician knew that the patient and his wife had thought about this for a long time. They had discussed it thoroughly. They were both resolute and determined to bring things to an end.

Finally after many days of agonizing thought, the physician arrived at a decision. He went to see the old couple and spoke with them. Having weighed all the pros and cons the physician had thought of a way that he could help them, a way that respected their rights as intelligent human beings to determine their own destiny. He would give them the knowledge that was necessary to make a safe decision and the future was in their hands, to do as they wished. Since he was leaving the country the next day, he informed the couple that he had left a prescription at the pharmacy for a month supply of narcotics and sleeping pills. He warned them of the danger of mixing pills and especially mixing pills and alcohol. He told them about attempted overdoses that had gone bad and the horrible consequences that could result. He warned them not to try it. He told them of a website where information on the effects of these drugs could be found; information as to what dosages were dangerous. And lastly he warned them of the dangers should they take more than what was prescribed. Satisfied that he had been understood, the physician said goodbye.

The loving couple always gracious thanked him for his wonderful care, and understanding. As he departed, he was given a warm embrace by the wife and with a tear in her eye and a soft voice she said a simple "thank you" and returned to the side of her bedridden husband. The next day the physician flew back to Newfoundland. Unfortunately or fortunately the physician never discovered what had become of the old couple, but he did feel that the few weeks spent with them had been the most educational and rewarding of his entire medical career.

Chapter XXII

IS THIS THE END?

Back on Perpetua most seekers accepted death and joined the organizations that filled their heads with false concepts of love and truth and so stress, pain and war became a permanent part of their daily lives. Sometimes a few seekers would genuinely search for the truth. Some would seek out the wise. Some would seek out the Oracles. Some would find answers in the journey of life. After spending years on the seas of confusion, laboring up the mountain of pain weighed down by their burden of vanity, greed, and intolerance many would find their journey hard. Some were able as they grew wiser in their search for truth, to lighten their load and shed these impediments. Finally reaching the lake of hope, they were able to see the island of tranquility, where they were able to drink from the fountain of knowledge with souls renewed by a newfound humility and gift of acceptance. For them the burden of death was banished and they were transformed becoming one with the cosmos. For most seekers however, especially the so called educated ones, truth was relative. Every truth was examined through a straw. Still most seekers were confused and could not see truth, especially when it came to religion and God.

God is an Elephant

After days of meetings all the great religions of Perpetua could still not agree on what God was. They did finally agree that God was really big and so they concluded that God was an Elephant, but they could not agree on what color he was. Looking through their straw one religious group saw the white of the elephant's eye and insisted God was white. Another religion looking at the elephants Iris insisted that God was blue. Looking at the elephants tongue anther religion insisted that God was decidedly pink. Looking at his skin through their straw, another religion adamantly insisted that God was grey.

No one accepted that maybe they were all partially right and all partially wrong. Maybe God was all of these and more that they could ever see. No one considered the fact that they were looking through straws. And so they argued and argued and each began to discredit the other. Respect for each other was lost and intolerance ended debate. They all left the meeting convinced that the other guy was wrong. Some even made it their mission to force into submission those who did not see it their way.

> *"It does not matter which end of the straw you look through,*
> *you are still looking through a straw."*
> Peter John Morry 2012

For eons throughout the universe sentient beings everywhere had pondered the meaning of life, death, God, time. No one had an answer. Many thought they knew. Few really understood the complexity of the constructs. Few believed in the cosmic consciousness. Few believed in transformation. Few understood death and most feared it.

This is it?

I lie here dying, my family all around me
Where did the time go? It cannot be
Where did it go? Is this it for me?

Eighty six years of what?
This baron soul, has God forgot?
Years of storms, and icy rain
Years of lonely, longing pain.

Struggles hard along the path,
Have left me filled with fear and wrath.
Alone I travelled inside my walls,
No answer to my mourning calls.

This shell that housed the aborted seed
Shuts out the world so I won't bleed.
Afraid to chance the broken dream
The arctic night is now my scene.

Regrets? My God! That's all there is.
Of things I failed to do.
Regrets of hurts I held within,
Of loves I never knew.

And now? I'm here on the Ledge Of things I do not know.
I'm out of time, with fear in mind
Of the place that I must go.

Terror! Terror! Fills my heart.
Afraid to close my eyes.
Into the darkness I depart,
As now I realize.

This is it!

This is it?

Some accepted simple explanations to the conundrum of creation, life, death, eternity, God, time. Some thought they had the answer, others only had questions.

MUSINGS

What is Life? Is there death after Life? Is Life intelligence? Is there intelligence after Life? Where does intelligence exist? Does intelligence exist as energy or as matter or as both? Is intelligence a thought? Can intelligence travel through space, through time? What is time? If time is the curvature of space, can time exist without space? Can space exist without time? Or are they one . . . Space-time? Why does time only move in one direction? Is it because the universe is expanding? Why is the universe expanding? What is it expanding from? Was there nothing before the big bang? If so how does something come from nothing? If there was something, was it energy or was it matter, and if so where did it exist? If it existed, what were its boundaries? For you must have boundaries to have existence. What did the boundaries consist of? Before the big bang when there was, no matter, no energy, no space, no time? What was there? If there was nothing, then what is nothing? Can you create something from nothing? Is nothing something? Was there anything before time? If nothing, then was there a God before time, before the big bang? If there was a God then where did he exist if there was nothing? Where did God come from? If God is not matter or not energy, then what is he? Is God intelligence? What is intelligence? Can intelligence exist outside the body, outside of time and space? Is intelligence matter or energy or something else? If something else what is it? Is intelligence the cosmic consciousness? Is that what God is?

Chapter XXIII

WHAT IS INTELLIGENCE?

The Oracle, seeing how much man had dominated and desecrated the planet, was curious about mans self image as an intelligent being. He was aware that man considered himself above the animals and even considered himself fashioned in the image of God. He was aware of the dangers inherent in setting oneself above. He had seen the consequences both on earth and in his own world of Perpetua. He decided to take Bill to seek out information on this topic.

He searched Wikipedia, the Library of Congress and several of the world's leading universities. He spoke to psychologists, anthropologists, engineers, archeologists, biochemists, biologists, philosophers, and men of the cloth and asked them all the same questions. "What is intelligence? Where does it reside inside the body or can it exist outside the body? What is it made of? Can you measure it? Can intelligence be teleported though space? Is intelligence a thought? Is it an energy wave like a radio wave or a light wave or does it travel in a frequency that man cannot yet measure? Does intelligence travel through space and time? Did intelligence exist before space and time? Does intelligence occupy space? Can intelligence travel through a vacuum? If it needs a medium to travel, what is that medium made of? Is intelligence moral or immoral or both? The rhythms of the earth such as the seasons, the tides, the water cycle, is that a form of intelligence? How do the trees know when to raise the sap and when to send it down? Is that intelligence? Individual plankton can come together from the ocean and form a colony, and then modify their own structure to form specialized functions within the colony. Is that intelligence? Ants in an ant colony have divisions of labor. Is that intelligence? The spermatozoa can seek and find an egg and then penetrate it starting new life. Is that intelligence? How does a cut know when to stop healing? Salmon can find their way home after travelling thousands of miles in the ocean for years? Is that intelligence? Homing pigeons find their way home from a thousand miles even if carried blinded in a box blind to their release point. Is that intelligence? The octopus and the dolphin have a bigger brain to body mass ratio than man. Does that make them more intelligent than man? Can these animals think existentially? We simply do not know. An eagle can see a mouse in the field from a mile in the sky. Whales can communicate over hundreds of miles using sonar and echo-location. Bats can fly at night using radar. Are all these signs of intelligence? Man cannot do these things. Are these animals therefore more intelligent than man? The dinosaurs dominated the planet for a hundred million years. Is survivability therefore a measure of intelligence? The shark, the turtle and the turkey are dinosaurs that are still with us. If survivability of the species is a sign of intelligence are they more intelligent than man?

The Oracle in his discussion with the intellectuals remarked that there were great men in all walks of life. Some were great artists, some great writers. There were great musicians, singers, philosophers, athletes, generals, and healers. He posed the question "are there different kinds of intelligence?"

The Oracle noted that mankind had considered himself special in the eyes of God because of his intelligence which he considered a gift from God. He asked "Were not all these forces mentioned above some form of Intelligence, and therefore special in the eyes of God?"

"The octopus has a bigger brain than man and has been around for hundreds of millions of years longer that man. An octopus, like the cuttlefish can change their color and appearance in an instant so that they blend perfectly into their environment and become invisible. Being so aware of its environment surely must mean that they must be more intelligent than man." One of the intellectuals commented as a rebuttal "If the octopus is so intelligent why has it not dominated the planet like man has? It cannot be as intelligent as man because it cannot reason." The Oracle commented in reply. "But how do we know the octopus has no ability to reason, to think about God, to think existentially" We do not know that he can't because we have no way of measuring its thoughts. Perhaps all living things can think existentially? We simply have no way of measuring intelligence. We do not even know what it is.

The scholar reiterated, "As I said before, if man is not the most intelligent creature on this planet why was he able to dominate the planet? Is that not because of his superior intelligence? With humor in his heart, the Oracle replied that perhaps man's domination of the planet could be considered a sign of man's lack of intelligence rather than a sign of his intelligence. He then continued his reply to the question from the scholar?

The Oracle then shared the following opinion: "From all my observations and all my readings I have concluded that mans impact on the planet is not solely due to his brain power because there are other creatures on the planet that have larger brains and therefore may be considered by some to be more intelligent than man. Man's impact on the planet has come from man's unique ability to make tools. Tools have been the instrument of man's domination of the planet. Man has evolved three major changes that have given him temporary dominance over the planet. He had evolved an opposed thumb which gives his hands the ability to make, hold and use tools and the ability to walk upright which frees his hands for use of these tools. The last great tool in mans evolutional is communication. Man has the ability to share his knowledge with other men through speech and writings. The combination of these attributes; communication, intelligence, hands, upright gate, and use of tools have made it possible for man to become the dominant species on earth. But most important of all is the fact that these attributes have made it possible for man to change his environment and change himself. This same mix, if not used properly, also makes it possible for him to insure his extinction on this earth as a species.

If man is as intelligent as he thinks he is he must find a way to insure his survival as a species. The first step on his journey of survival is for man to become less arrogant and to recognize that he is not special, and not above nature. Man is a part of nature and cannot control it. He may exert influence upon it but in the end nature will dominate all. All creatures of nature are part of a web and are so interdependent on each other that what affects one will somehow affect another. The principle of *The Butterfly Effect* embraces this concept. To survive we must adapt to change which is inevitable. The strength of nature is in diversity not sameness. All creations by being a part of that web are special. The more knowledge man possesses the more adaptable he will become. ***Change is the only constant in the Universe.*** Failure to change is the Path to extinction and adaptability to change is the engine of survival. We must embrace change not fear it."

"Because of the fact that, 'the more we know the more we realize we don't know', we can reach only one conclusion and that is: "***Intelligence therefore is the ability to acquire knowledge and to use that knowledge to adapt to change.***"

"If man has a chance for survival as a species he must keep an open free society where complete access to knowledge is the right of every human being. Any departure from this principle, no matter how miniscule diminishes his chances of survival as a species. *There are no answers there are only questions.*"

For those who heard the oracle and understood the message of love and oneness of God, man, and nature and as a result became transformed the following poems are more appropriate.

"What is God?"

What is God?
For some God is a force out there, somewhere,
overseeing the entire universe with a personal interest in them?
For others, God is a part of everything and therefore
is not outside looking in, but is inside looking out
and asking them "how are they doing?"
Peter J Morry 2011

River of Time

My Journey is coming to an End.
The River that is my world rushes somewhere.
I am only a molecule in a sea of molecules,
Racing somewhere, coming from somewhere.
Like the water molecule, I know not what came before,
Nor what will come after. I do not even know my banks,
my bottom, my sky.

I only know that I am here, wherever that is, in a world that is one;
With no countries, no borders, no languages.
I am here. This is now. Where is my meaning?

Sometimes I am a mist, sometimes a cloud, sometimes a raindrop,
sometimes a river, sometimes a lake, sometimes an ocean. Great as the
ocean is, I am still only one among many.
I bring life to the animals, trees, grasses, earth.
For without me there is nothing.
I bring beauty, solitude, tranquility and storms.
I am a creator, a destroyer, a builder, a nurturer.
I am eternal.
I am God!

Chapter XXIV

THE CROSSROADS

The Oracle had come to Earth to investigate the discordant wave of energy that had disturbed him back on the planet Perpetua many galaxies away in another universe. The wave of energy had emanated from planes flying into buildings killing thousands of souls and the subsequent consequences unleashed by that event would ripple around planet Earth for over one hundred years. For that event marked the beginning of the end of society as mankind had known it.

The event had been perpetrated by power seekers, looking to draw various nations into a conflict from which they could benefit economically. If would precipitate a war that would lead to the economic collapse of one of the most powerful nations on earth. The economic consequences of the wars that followed would plunge the whole world into a deep depression that would last thirty years. The same scenario had been run many times before in the history of planet Earth. A series of such false flag events had led one of the most powerful nations on earth into a series of conflicts that bled it dry both spiritually and economically. Because of these wars, a country that had once led the world in freedom was now enslaved by the shackles of economic ruin. Everywhere people felt threatened; everywhere people thought terrorists were trying to destroy their way of life. People were willing to sacrifice their freedoms for security, and as a consequence ended up with neither. The beginning of the end was near. They were at a crossroad. If the right decision was not made and made soon the world would descend into financial and social ruin that would last a hundred years. There would be mass starvation, riots, wars and devastation. All social institutions would break down. The eleventh hour was drawing near. Radical changes needed to be made before it was too late.

About a century earlier, the power seekers had convinced the most powerful nations on earth to go to a Fiat money system, in which money could be printed out of thin air. By doing that the government had betrayed their people, for not only had they given bankers the power to arbitrarily print money but they also had given the bankers sole stewardship over it. That mistake would eventually cost everyone their freedom and lead to a one world government by the banksters. They had created a world that was Orwellian in nature.

> *"Allow me to issue and control the money of a nation*
> *and I care not who makes the Laws"*
> Mayer Amschel Rothschild 1828

For a century, the system had allowed people to live beyond their means, and to amass large debts. The system had allowed countries to wage wars that they could not afford. Eventually everyone was broke, except of course the power seekers, who could print money at will and acquire assets and wealth from the warring nations. The masses were unaware of the construct that that in war the only winners were the bankers. In every area the banksters drained the people of their money. They were able to manipulate the stock markets and when they crashed, they made money on the way up and on the way down. The banksters had convinced everyone that they needed things, that possessions were good, that sharing was bad, that the enemy was the other guy. The entire world was in debt to the banksters and the world had become unstable, and cooperation among nations and amongst people within nations began to disappear. Blacks were suspicious of whites, whites were suspicious of blacks, and everyone distrusted their institutions, and with good reason too. Everywhere there was corruption.

Politicians were corrupt. The judiciary could be bought. Elections were rigged. Media propagandized. Constitutions were trashed by politicians. Freedoms were curtailed. Religions preached love, peace, charity but their hypocrisy became exposed and were no longer trusted. Sexual abuse was rampant among the clergy, amongst the Boy Scouts. Who was left to trust? Was there anybody you could trust? People fell away from their churches, as belief in these institutions waned. Electronic balloting which could be altered by those in power had robbed the people of their democracy. Mass media was owned by the corporations, and lies became the truth. Those that really did tell the truth were ignored by the media, and the money masters used their power to promote the message of fear, and intolerance. Only a few understood what was happening and could see the future which was a world dominated by a handful of psychopaths.

These few who tried to expose the truth were discredited as *Conspiracy Theorists* by the corporate media and the masses of people refused to believe them. The truth was too scary to contemplate and the truth seekers, labeled as conspiracy theorists, were dismissed. Anyone who dissented anywhere from the mantra of Big Brother was labeled a terrorist, and was placed in prisons without trial. Principles of justice that had been in place for a thousand years were replaced by presidential edict. People were no longer considered innocent until proven guilty. No one had a right to a fair trial of their peers. Show trials that were staged by the Power Seekers were common, but there was no justice. Dissenters sometimes were not even imprisoned; they were simply blown up by drones. Thousands of innocent people were killed. Everywhere people were in denial. When they were told that their neighbor was a terrorist by their government they did not question it. They did not realize that the terrorist was their government.

The vision of the future was so frightening that people discredited the messengers as the evil ones. Cameras, drones, and spyware in computers, cars, and cell phones were tracking peoples every move. Plans were being made to put computer tracking chips in people's bodies at birth, all in the name of security. People were told that the chips would make them safer. Drones would patrol the skies and privacy would not exist. Children would be taught to inform on their parents and all access to information would be controlled by the state. Plastic cards would replace paper money and credit could be cancelled at will by the state. People would be housed in concentration (FEMA) camps to protect them from terrorists who they were told were everywhere. People got poorer and poorer trying to pay for all this security and finally recreation was limited to one hour per day.

In the beginning most people refused to believe the truth when they were told it, by the few who were smart enough to see it. For many, many, years great men had warned about the dangers of maintaining standing armies, of the military-industrial complex, and secret societies. Mahatma Gandhi, Nelson Mandela, Dwight D Eisenhower, John F. Kennedy, Robert Kennedy, Martin Luther King, George Orwell, were some of the many men that had seen the writing on the wall and tried to change things for the better. Some of them were killed for their beliefs. A few people heard and understood their message, but most people ignored it, and as a result the money masters and the power seekers had had their way. Things continued to deteriorate for all the people on earth.

But the system was gradually faltering under its own weight of corruption and greed and eventually would collapse. Stagnation and not evolution became the operant force. This policy of consumerism and greed as explained before was against the laws of nature and would eventually lead to a total collapse of the system. Perhaps it was coming too late, but there was no doubt change would be coming. It had to. The system of power and greed was unsustainable. The Oracle observed that the same sequence of events was happening back in his beloved Perpetua. The parallels were frightening.

Web of Deceit

Nobody takes the time to read the signs.
Instead, together, we follow the web into the twine.
Planned experience everywhere all around,
Define the matrix by which we're bound.
Predetermined paths insure we do not stray,
While beyond the web, hidden masters prey.
With ever present, overseeing eyes, our masters
Execute the plan for our demise.

Like trapped fish we swim round and round, following each other,
Oblivious to the fact, we all have been here before.
It matters not where we go, nor from whence we came,
Only that together we play the game.
We know that where we are is not the place to be,
And the wider picture we do not see.
But still we do not fear, because we move as one,
Content to keep on moving until we are undone.

We fear when someone strikes a different path.
With contempt we pressure them and show our wrath.
We wave the flag, question loyalty,
Patriotism, honor, insures conformity.

In an instant the net is raised out of the water,
And we realize . . . . we are all . . . . undone.

**"None are more hopelessly enslaved,
than those who falsely believe they are free"**
Johann *Wolfgang van Goethe*

Chapter XXV

"ON GOOD AND EVIL"

Isa 59:14-15 Justice is turned back, and righteousness stands afar off; For truth is fallen in the street, and equity cannot enter.
: 15 so truth fails, and he [who] departs from evil makes himself a prey. Then the LORD saw [it], and it displeased Him that [there was] no justice.

The Oracle was amazed by all the killing and hatred that he saw in the world during his travels. TV was full of violence. Children's electronic games were steeped in violence. Politicians wrapped themselves in blankets of religion, and tripped over themselves trying to appear more holy than their opponent. At the same time, the same politicians, were promoting war; invading this country and bombing that one. Financial disaster was just around the corner, yet the politicians were talking about increasing military spending. They wanted to cut all the social programs. Give the rich more tax breaks to stimulate the economy, and take more from the poor such as health care. Social programs must go. We must remain safe. Build more walls. Build more bombs. Build more nuclear weapons. Don't let anyone else have them, for we are the chosen people. Only we have the right to rule the world. The history of the world was filled with nations that thought like that and all their empires came crashing down. The most recent empire that came crashing down was supposed to last one thousand years, yet only lasted six. And now another empire was crumbling. Mankind had become obsessed with war and killing. Their new God had become greed. They did not realize that the real enemy was not outside but inside themselves. They did not realize that the money masters and the power seekers had brainwashed them, had enslaved them.

The Oracle decided to take Bill to visit a philosophy class at a nearby University. The question of the day was. ***Is the concept of "Good and Evil" genetically encoded or learned."*** The debate was fascinating. The Oracle listened to arguments from both sides. The end result was no one could agree, but one particular speaker had developed a theory that the Oracle found interesting.

This speaker was an old man of seventy. He explained that he had no political affiliation but had been a world traveler for forty years. He considered himself a citizen of the world and a philosopher at heart. He said that he had no formal education in philosophy but in his travels and from his readings he had formed some radical world views. He said that he felt that it was important that they be discussed. He felt that he had a moral obligation to his fellow man to put forward his views. He then went on to speak. What he had to say was as follows.

He said; "My readings had taught me that the universe as a whole was made up of two main ingredients matter and energy. There was nothing else. They were interchangeable as Einstein had shown with his equation; $E = MC\ squared$. One was either matter or energy. And the conversion back and forth between the two was going on, every second everywhere in the Universe. The total amount of matter and energy in the Universe was constant. There was no such thing as the forces of good or the forces of evil. There was only the force of creation or the force of destruction as matter and energy were inter-convertible. These forces were operant everywhere, in every molecule, in every structure, in every form of matter and in every form of energy. They were active in every creature on earth and in everything these creatures created, including societies. The creatures and societies that had the right balance of these forces of creation and destruction were successful and were stable for a while, but eventually the balance of these forces would shift and a metamorphosis into another form would occur. Nothing is lost or gained on the molecular level. The only thing that changes is the form. The proportion of each ingredient 'matter or energy' in this new metamorphic entity would determine its form."

"How that form interacts with other forms around it, will determine its stability and its longevity. That new metamorphic form interacts with its environment and its environment interacts with it. The interaction changes both, both the form and its environment. If the form can adapt to the charges occurring in the environment it will evolve and have endurance. Implicit within this process of evolving is the ability to change and adapt. Forms that cannot adapt to change become extinct. The same is true of societies."

"So *the main driving force of nature is not good and evil, but creation and destruction, and the ability to adapt*. This concept Charles Darwin called *"the survival of the fittest*." The only constant in nature is change. This is the force that Darwin called *"evolution."* Animals, plants, mountains, oceans, planets, stars, galaxies, universes are never constant. They are always changing. Eventually all will be destroyed and reborn in some new transformation. Societies and the laws that govern societies are always changing. Those laws and societies can only survive if they can adapt. We must embrace and accept change if we are to survive. Sick societies fear change. The institutions of society by and large are static. They resist change because they are run by the power seekers and the money masters. They want to keep their power and therefore resist change. Therefore since they are fighting the forces of evolution they will all eventually die and another form will take its place. Consider a volcano, if there is not a gradual release of the pent up forces of change through venting there will eventually be a cataclysmic eruption in which the whole mountain and the environment around it will be destroyed; a better word is morphed, since nothing in nature is destroyed it merely changes form. So too it is in societies."

"But what of good and evil? The forces of good and evil do not exist in nature. Let me repeat. **The forces of good and evil do not exist in nature; there is only the force of change**. Good and evil are constructs defined by man. They are moral imperatives that man created to regulate societies or enhance power and wealth. There is nothing immoral about a lion killing a gazelle. That is an expression of the natural application of the law of *the survival of the fittest*. The same is true of a lion killing another lion to protect his pride or food he needs for survival."

"The same can be said in the case of humans. When it is a matter of life and death of survival, it is not immoral to kill if that is the only option. Only in that instance is it natural and not immoral. But it must clearly be the only option. It must be the last resort. If it is not clearly the only option then it is immoral. For instance to declare war or to kill simply because someone has a different form of government i.e. communism versus capitalism is clearly immoral. It is not the only choice, and the rights of others to believe differently must be respected. To declare war because someone has a resource that we feel we need is clearly immoral. Not having oil is for instance, not a life and death issue. It is a financial issue. We cannot take someone's oil simply because we need it for financial reasons. What gives us that right? We simply do not have it."

"Man is the only creature on earth that claims ownership of his surroundings. Lions don't put up fences. Man has this sense of entitlement. Nowhere else in nature does that phenomenon occur! This clearly is not a matter of survival but a matter of perceived rights and falls under the category of moral law, and not natural law. Killing in this instance is immoral because man does not have a right to own nature. Ownership is a manmade construct and is not subject to the principles of Natural law but to the principals of moral law. The North American Indian knew this and believed that man could not own the earth. However if possession of something that is needed for survival of life is involved it becomes an issue of Natural law. Having access to water may be such an issue. If we need water for survival and we do not have it, do we have the right to take it? It depends on the circumstances. For instance if we chose to live in the dessert where there is no water and where there never was water does that give us the right to kill our neighbor and steal his water? Clearly no, but if we are living in a fertile valley and where there has always been water and someone upstream diverts our water supply and steals our water so that we can no longer survive, then we have the right to protect our water by force if necessary, and only then if that is the last resort. If there is an abundance of water, more than they need, the lucky ones have a moral obligation to share with their less fortunate brethren. If there is not enough for their own needs then they have the right to secure a fair share and defend that right by violence if necessary. But who then decides how much is enough? Even then it still is not that simple."

"Let me give an example of what on the surface might seem like a simple case, but in reality still is not black and white."

"Suppose you are in an airplane with one other person. You are at 50,000 feet. The pilot takes a heart attack and dies, and the plane goes into a potentially fatal dive. There is only one parachute and there are two of you. Your companion grabs the parachute first and refuses to share it with you. The plane is descending rapidly. You grab a steel bar and beat him to death. Are you guilty of murder? Or is this a clear case of the application of the natural law of nature, "the survival of the fittest". Should that man if he survives be tried for murder? The answer is most definitely yes! Is he guilty of murder?

Maybe! Some may say immediately yes. Others might immediately say no. That is why we need a trial. Is this a simple case of the survival of the fittest; a case where natural law applies? Or is this a case of murder, where moral law applies? First, we must determine if this was the only option since under moral law killing should always be the last resort. Was that the only option? Was that the last resort? That is what has to be decided in a court of law. What facts need to be considered? I will list a few just to clarify the point that nothing is ever black and white. There are always shades of grey. Invariably people who take extreme points of view are never right."

"There are very few absolutes in nature. The practice of abortion is such an issue. Every case is different and each instance needs to be considered on its own merit. To illustrate this principle I have chosen a supposedly simpler case but in reality it is very complicated."

"What if it could be determined that, both men sharing the same parachute had a 100% chance of survival? What if while sharing the parachute the chances of survival were 75%. How about 50% or 25% or zero. What if it could be determined that the survivor knew that the answer was 100% and took it anyway? What if he did not know? What if it was determined that the survivor had been an expert at flying planes on video games, and had a reasonable chance of successfully flying the plane and chose not to? What if the victim had such skill and was killed before he had a chance to explore that option? What if the survivor was 60 yrs old, dying of cancer and had six months to live and the victim age 20 was healthy? What if the victim was dying of cancer? What if the victim was on the verge of finding a cure for cancer; a cure that could save millions of people? What if the survivor was such a person? What if the victim was Adolph Hitler, a rapist, or a child abuser? What if the survivor was one of these? What if the survivor was wealthy and promised to give millions of dollars, to the poor if he was found innocent? What if the survivor had a gene in him that guaranteed a cure for Aids, and he refused to share it if he was found guilty. What if the victim had that same gene and the survivor didn't? As you can see the list of things that can make this an immoral act is legion."

"Perhaps yet a simpler example should be given. You are in a combat and your fellow soldier has secret information that if extracted by the enemy could cost thousands of lives. You have only one bullet left and it is almost certain that you both will be captured alive. You shoot your friend with your only bullet. Is that murder?"

"Let's return to the original question, *what is good and evil*?"

"As I said above, I do not believe that good and evil are forces of nature. I firmly believe that they do not exist at all. What does exist is the natural force of survival of the fittest. Good and evil are constructs that man has created to give the societies that he has created survival value. Good and evil are moral imperatives invented by man to define behavior. The highest forms of these imperatives are codified into laws. Religions are another form of rules and regulations invented by man to control behavior. Laws and organized religions have been largely corrupted by power and are in a large part dysfunctional. What is most important in man is the instinct for survival that has been passed down and modified in his genes through the process of natural selection over millions of years."

"This process has given him an innate sense of morality that has allowed him to survive and evolve as a species. Since Mother Nature works on probabilities as is now becoming clearer in string theory, there are also encoded in his genes destructive forces as well. Hence the existence of such creatures as Adolf Hitler, Joseph Stalin and other war mongers of the world that have been responsible for millions of deaths. Taking the logic a step further we can conclude that most if not all wars are immoral and can never be justified under any circumstances. The same can be said of using the death penalty in our justice system. It simply is not the last resort."

"Recently experiments with babies as young as six months of age have shown that even at that age babies have a sense of morality, a sense of what we would call right or wrong. However those are bad words to use because like the word *God* everyone has a different sense of what they mean; therefore I use them reluctantly. That sense of morality is innate and is encoded in our genes. Fortunately for mankind, the genes for behavior that have survival value have so far outweighed the effects of the genes that have destructive potential. That is why we are still here after millions of years. What worries me is that situation may soon change."

"As mentioned before change is constant, and adaptation is critical to survival. If we don't adapt to the change we simply will not survive. In the last 100 years mankind has done more to destroy his environment that he has done in the previous five million of his existence combined. Our population is approaching seven billion. One hundred years ago before the discovery of oil it was less than five hundred million. Our impact on our environment is so monumental that the argument can be made that our survival as a species is in danger. Science has determined that of all the life forms that have ever existed on this planet since its formation, approximately 99.9999% have already become extinct. So will we in time. The question is not if we will become extinct but when. I suspect that if we don't change our current course of action it will be sooner rather than later."

"Some of the supremacists out there argue that there should be a human cull. Many countries have developed weapons of mass destruction much more serious and deadly than the atomic bomb. I speak of course of germ warfare. Some countries have given themselves the status of the rulers of the world. They have given themselves a sense of entitlement. "They have the right to determine who can have nuclear weapons and who should not."

"In an over populated world, will this same logic be used to determine who should live and who should not? All the chosen ones have to do is vaccinate themselves and then release a deadly germ such as the Ebola virus and those non-vaccinated would die? Are there people crazy enough to do this? Of course there are! Do we need large armies to protect ourselves from such people? Of course not! The only reason for large armies is to generate money for the money masters and to keep everyone enslaved through poverty. The only protection we need is protection from ourselves for the enemy lies within. ***All we need is to do is to destroy that sense of entitlement that gives us the "We versus them" mentality.*** How do we do that? We must restore power to the people and we do that through enlightenment not entitlement."

Chapter XXVI

THE SOLUTION

The solution to the future survivability of mankind as a species given the challenges of the modern world had become clear to the Oracle. As discussed above, the greatest constant in nature is change. Societies as currently constructed are designed to resist change not embrace it. The driving force of evolution is change. Darwin has clearly shown that those who resist change are doomed to extinction. Man as a species and as an individual has to undergo an absolute mind boggling change in our individual and collective thinking if we are to survive. The concept of "Me first" which is so ingrained in our society must become the concept of "We first." The word "them" must be struck from our vocabulary. Currently the power seekers and the money masters have the whole world on the verge of moral, social, and financial bankruptcy.

Democracy is dysfunctional everywhere, because the will of the people is not being expressed in action. In fact it is not even being heard because the mass media has been corrupted and are censoring the few voices of reason that are out there. People seem to forget that the mass media are owned by the power seekers. Mass media are not democratic. Their purpose is not to inform but to ensure that we conform. They are driven by the profit construct, not the sharing construct. Mass media is an instrument used to fight change and maintain the inequities of the current power structure. Proof that they are succeeding in their intention is evidenced by the fact that "the rich keep getting richer and the poor keep getting poorer. Intolerance and distrust are everywhere and everyone is afraid. People can't trust their governments, churches, justice system (i.e. the Warren Commission). The integrity of our electoral system is now compromised more than ever. Electronic voting has insured that it is now easier to rig elections. Politicians cannot be trusted, probably never should have been, but it is now worse than ever. Politicians need vast wealth to get elected to high office. Where does this wealth come from? Do not the politicians have allegiance to their rich benefactors rather than to the people at large? If there was an honest politician who was advocating massive structural change, changing our institutions, giving power to the people, redistributing wealth, etc., would he get the air time from the mass media and the very institutions he was trying to change? Certainly Not! *"Power corrupts and absolute power corrupts absolutely."*

CHANGES WE CAN MAKE

So *what can we do given the corruption all around us*, was the question the Oracle put to the assembly of scholars and was the subject of much heated debate. They, after days of discussion and deliberation, the assembly came up with the following recommendations.

1. The first change has to occur within ourselves. We must embrace the concept of spaceship earth and its inherent conclusion that we are all in this together and will sink or swim together. We cannot change anything until we change ourselves first.

2. The next thing we must do is protect the Internet at all costs. It is the best vehicle for sharing knowledge that we now possess, and it is worldwide.

3. Next we must use antitrust legislation to bust up the power of large financial intuitions and the corporate media.

4. We must ban all electronic voting, that is not supported by a paper trail.

5. We must force all politicians to declare every penny of their campaign contributions. We must put a limit on the amount of campaign contributions in an election and ban all corporate contributions altogether. This is so important that it should be declared an act of treason to break this law.

6. We should ban all professional lobbyists. No x-politician should be allowed to become a lobbyist

7. We should give all political candidates equal and free air time.

8. All candidates should be allowed only two terms in office.

9. No relative of any candidate should be allowed to belong to any organization that is involved in the election process.

10. Any form of election fraud no matter how trivial should be considered an act of treason.

11. Every elected government official should have the right to vote his or her conscience on all legislation irrespective of party affiliation. To enable this to happen we need to elect all cabinet ministers to their particular portfolios. For instance any member from any party can run for finance minister or education minister etc. The elected cabinet should work like a corporate board and decide on policies independent of party affiliation. The house as a whole should vote on policies developed by government. The defeat of legislation should not mean the defeat of the government. The prime minister or president should function solely as chairman of the board and can have extraordinary powers only at the discretion of the cabinet. He cannot fire a cabinet minister without approval of 2/3rds of the cabinet. All members of Parliament can be recalled by a referendum for due cause.

    The format for this recall should be fully democratic and independent of parliamentary control.

12. There should be no such concept as voting along party lines. Every vote should be free and independent.

13. There should be better and stronger laws in place to protect whistle blowers.

14. Every candidate that runs for political office should have representative voting power according to his percentage of the popular vote he received.

15. Politicians accepting bribes should be charged with high treason.

16. An ethics board should be elected in every election cycle and should review all legislation before it is written into law and their recommendations should be made public before a vote is allowed. Only highly educated people with knowledge of the principles of ethics, finances, and justice should be allowed to chair such boards and there should be representatives from all walks of society on such boards.

17. All omnibus bills should be banned. No bills should be bundled and all bills should be passed individually on their own merit.

18. The Fiat Money System should be banned and there should be a return to the gold standard.

19. There should be a limit placed on the size of banks and all banks should have strict controls on the kinds of investments they make.

20. All media should be under control of an elected board responsible to the judiciary, and the size of all media should be limited.

21. Budgets should be balanced every year, except in extraordinary times and approved by a 2/3 majority of cabinet, and a 51% majority of Parliament.

22. Churches should not be allowed to contribute financially to any politician or political institution or organization and should be taxed.

23. Ethics programs and courses should be made mandatory in schools and should be aired free of charge on all mass media outlets on a regular basis. Tax credits should be given to people who watch

these programs and show some proof of understanding the basic principles of ethics and justice.

24. We should keep the one person one vote system.

25. Anyone with a criminal record should forfeit their right to vote for five years after discharge from prison

26. All soldiers should be given the right to refuse to fight without penalty if they are valid conscientious objectors.

27. In times of peace, military budgets should be slashed to 10% of the GNP. This should be overseen by the UN with powers to penalize offenders.

28. No country should have the right of veto in the United Nations, and there should be no permanent members on the Security Council.

29. The weaponization of space should be banned.

30. All Countries should have the right to have nuclear weapons, and no country should have the right to possess more than five such weapons in their arsenal at any one time.

31. All classified documents should be available for scrutiny after 10 years through an enhanced freedom of information act. It should be considered an act of treason destroy any classified document without prior consent of a 2/3 majority of the general body of parliament.

32. Secrecy and secret societies should be considered a menace to society. Anyone having been a member of such a society should be banned from running for public office. Anyone found to be a member of a secret society should be charged with sedition and tried accordingly.

33. The CIA and such organizations should be disbanded in times of peace.

34. Certified volunteerism to preapproved organizations should be given a tax credit. All education should be free.

The assembly then decided that they would take the recommendations listed above as talking points with the view of totally overhauling societies all over the world. They would try to organize more symposia worldwide and maybe reach some form of consensus, a tall order indeed. This consensus many considered impossible to achieve but they all agreed that there was a need to create awareness of the evils that were destroying societies worldwide. Should they fail to do this and allow the gap between the rich and poor to continue then societies the world over were doomed and eventually perhaps man as a species?"

Chapter XXVII

THE MOST FUNDAMENTAL CHANGE OF ALL

Having looked all societies all over the world and having consulted with many scholars the Oracle asked to address the assembly again. He had one final suggestion, which he considered the most fundamental of all. Assuming the role of a Philosopher he addressed the assembly and spoke, as if he were a human using the knowledge he had acquired in his travels over the entire world.

He realized that what he was about to say would probably cause an uproar and may indeed destroy the small consensus that had been achieved with so much difficulty during the preceding discussions. He knew that it was a great risk but it was a risk he had to take. For he believed that if the change he was about to propose did not occur, then in reality nothing would change, and all would be lost. He cleared his throat and with bated breath addressed the assembly. Within seconds of speaking he could sense the resistance in the audience. Nevertheless he spoke clearly and with conviction. He had this to say

"The most fundamental change of all, the one that can most affect the ability to change our societies and ourselves, is our concept of God. Let me put it another way. People must change their fundamental concept of God. This is the most significant change of all because the concept of God affects the way people view the world and everything in it. Without this fundamental change in thinking, no real or lasting change in fact is possible. Let me explain, but first I need to state that the root of all evil is greed and greed comes from the way people view

God and their relationship with God. Now before I go any further, let me define greed."

"Greed is an excessive desire to possess wealth, goods, or abstract things of value with the intention to keep it for one's self. It is applied to a very excessive or rapacious desire and pursuit of wealth, status, and power."

"As a secular psychological concept, *greed is an inordinate desire to acquire or possess more than one needs or deserves.* It is typically used to criticize those who seek excessive material wealth, although it may apply to the need to feel excessively more moral, more socially important, or otherwise better than someone else."

"Where does greed come from? Do not our religions tell us to love thy neighbor as thyself? Should we not then be sharing? Where does the concept of ownership of property come from? From where comes the sense that mankind is special; that he is special in the eyes of God? That he is above the other creatures of the earth? Is it because he has been given freewill, supposedly by God, that man is special? Isn't he made in the image of God? Isn't he Godlike? That is what most of our religions tell us. And therein lays the problem. Mankind by putting himself intellectually above nature has divorced himself from nature."

"What is freewill anyway, this special something that man thinks he has and no other creature has? Do not the lions choose which Gazelle they will single out and eat? Is that not freewill? What then is freewill. If freewill is the ability to reason then it also means that man has also be given the ability to be unreasonable. Using choices that man has made, using that ability to reason, will determined what we will become as a species. The so called progress we have made. Technology then is a result of the ability to reason. Could it be that freewill is not a gift from without i.e. an external God, but is instead a gift from within i.e. from our genes? It makes more sense to believe that freewill (the ability to reason) is an evolutionary force that has been gradually developed as we evolved from the apes; than to think that it was suddenly imposed on us from without. To believe that it was imposed from without begs the question "On what day did this happen?" On what day did man stop being an ape and become godlike?

The concept that "one day man could not reason and the next day he could is much harder to accept since it implicitly rejects all of evolutionary theory. It makes more sense to consider that the ability to reason has evolved with us as we have evolved as a species"

"Could it be that mankind confuses freewill (the ability to reason) with technology? Is it not technology that has made us different from other creatures on the planet and not freewill? The concept that the ability to reason has been responsible for all of the advances of mankind is fundamentally sound. But it is also reasonable to assume that the ability to reason is also responsible for all the destructive forces that have been released on nature by man."

"The concept that man has been given the ability to reason by an external God that exists outside of man is fundamentally a toxic one. Man has been led to believe that he has been created in God's image and therefore unlike the other creatures on earth is special. Is that not a good thing? How is that toxic? On the surface it looks benign enough. In fact it looks great."

"The belief that we are godlike can be used by people to make them feel good and to foster good behavior, because everyone has been told that God is good and God is just. Therefore by making ourselves godlike; are we not aspiring to the concepts of goodness and justice? Surely that must be good! That may be so, but there is poison in the brew. The fly in the ointment is that by aspiring to be godlike we have also given ourselves a sense of superiority and entitlement. That sense of superiority and entitlement has resulted in our distancing ourselves from Mother Nature, and has spawned what has always been the greatest scourge of mankind, and that is the belief that we are above nature. Nature is here for us to conquer, for us to use, for us to possess, for us to own. This sense of ownership and entitlement fosters a sense of greed and leads to abuse."

"Greed is the source of all dysfunction in our society. It always has and always will be so. Greed leads to stratification of societies. As resources are unevenly accumulated and distributed we get hierarchies of power and wealth. We get the reinforcement of the sense of entitlement and ownership. We get the "us versus them" mentality. Hierarchies breed greed. *"He who has much wants more."* Greed breeds indifference and intolerance. Indifference and intolerance lead to suspicion and mistrust. Suspicion and mistrust lead to fear. Fear leads to territoriality and patriotism. Territoriality and patriotism almost certainly lead to war."

"What we need is fundamental change at the very soul of human nature. We need to take the lens with which we view the world and ourselves and smash it into a million pieces. We need to stop thinking of God as being above everything. God is not above everything. God is in everything. God is in us. God is us. We are God. We are not special. Everything is special. When we destroy a piece of nature we destroy a piece of ourselves. We destroy a piece of God. God did not create the Universe. God is the Universe and Everything in it. Because the Universe is ever changing God is ever changing, not everlasting. God is nature. If we want to be one with God we must be one with Nature."

"I repeat God is in us. God is in everything. To believe that God is inside looking out, and not outside looking in, is a fundamental change in thinking. It does not make God less potent, but in fact, makes him more potent for now God is aware of our every heartbeat, every breath, and every thought. Knowing that and more important feeling that God exists inside of us makes it easier to have a personal relationship with God and with others since the God we know is inside of them too. It also has the effect of placing all of God's creatures on the same level. Believing that God is in everything means that there is no hierarchy, no power difference between us and all of nature; therefore the abuse of nature should not occur. Man and nature will be equal in respect and love."

"We do not have to deny the existence of God as we know him to make this fundamental shift in belief. We only have to make a fundamental shift in where we believe he resides. Does God reside out there somewhere looking in or does God reside inside looking out? As stated previously God is everywhere. God is in everything. Everything is God. By redefining our view of what God is and where he resides we can get people to realize that we are one with nature and change our behavior towards nature. Therein is the solution. To deny that God exists is about as silly as denying Nature exists, or that the world exists, or that the Universe exists, for god is all of these. God is that fundamental force of creation and recreation that is the circle of life, which is our Universe. Note I said *which is our Universe* and not which exists in our Universe. There is a huge conceptual difference in meaning here. Since everything in the Universe is God, and everything in the Universe is constantly changing, everything in the Universe is alive. The circle of life is the circle of everything rocks, trees, everything."

"The universe is so vast, that every object in it seems to be at its center. We can only get to know a small part of our Universe, and given the limits of our senses, we can only get to know a miniscule part of that miniscule part. Most of it we cannot see, so we draw conclusions about the entire Universe based on the small part that we can see. There is much to be discovered, it is as if we are looking at only one grain of sand and making our assumptions about the entire universe from that one grain. There is certainly room for error here and room for change and growth in our knowledge. So it is with God. God is so vast that we all have different views of what he is; our view of what he is depends on what part of his universe we see. No one can see all of it. Such is the reality of God. So the only part of God that we can truly get to know and understand is the part that is inside of us. That is why we must learn to view God from an inside out approach. We must view God as inside of us looking out, and not outside looking in. In essence then God is our conscience and we are closest to god when we do what is correct for survival of ourselves and the world we live in. Because most humans have almost identical genes we as humans are more alike than different. Our ability to understand one another and thereby love and trust one another is easier if we believe that a part of God resides in each and every one of us."

The differences that separate mankind, pale in comparison to the similarities that unite us"
P. J. Morry 2012

"It should be stated that the belief that God resides within us does not mean that God dies with us when we die. Nothing disappears or is lost with death. God is not diminished with our death, nor is God enhanced by our birth. Since the amount of matter and energy in the Universe is constant (E=MC squared). All death and life means is that the sum total of what we are has not changed it merely has changed form or in other words evolved into something else. The force of evolution then is merely the force of God changing form. *Life and death then are merely God changing form.*"

"And what of heaven and hell? Do they exist and if so where are they. Of course heaven and hell exist. They exist inside of every one of us. If we love ourselves and are in harmony with nature then we are with God, for God is in us. If heaven means being with God then we are in Heaven. Hell by extension is also within us if we are in disharmony with ourselves or nature. If we do not love ourselves and others then we are in Hell."

"And what of death and life after death, do they exist; most definitely not. There is no death. Since there is no death there is no life after death. There is only Life and Transformation. Since the amount of matter and energy (Life) in the Universe is constant, there is only transformation.

"In the entire Universe *there is no death. There is only creation and recreation*".

"By redefining our concept of God in this manner, by recognizing that we humans are a small part of what God is, as is every other creature in creation, we are all star dust, and therefore the conceptual distance that we have created between "Us and them" should eventually disappear and our respect for each other and our environment should improve. Since happiness is easier to find if we are taught to love ourselves and to love others as ourselves, cooperation between humans should be easier to attain".

The Oracle concluded his presentation. There was no applause. No one knew what to say. The moderator after about 20 seconds of silence called out "Next Speaker Please."

The Oracle continued to listen to the presentations of others. Few of the others had any real insights into the realities of the situation. The next day, in the newspapers and on the TV, the radical speaker or his comments were not mentioned. It was as if it never happened. But the Oracle knew and understood and there were many more enlightened people like the world traveler out there. After all the potential for good and evil was in everyone. Man as a species just needed to be enlightened. Perhaps things could change. Perhaps things would change. They must.

Chapter XXVIII

GOING HOME

It was time to go home. The Oracle had had a very informative visit to earth in his quest for truth and enlightenment. The lesions that he had learned on earth could have application in his own world of Perpetua. Similar things were happening there. The words of the world traveler had resonated with him. He went over again the things he had learned in his mind.

The Oracle could see that the world had got themselves into a gigantic mess. It would take a colossal restructuring of society to bring about change. All sentient beings were Seekers. They were not born with greed, intolerance, bigotry, hatred. These were all learned behaviors, not genetically encoded. Behaviors learned from society. If real change were to occur those behaviors would have to be unlearned. How can they be unlearned?

The Oracle knew that most institutions in existence on earth and in Perpetua were motivated to preserve the existing power structure. Differences in knowledge meant difference in power. To avoid the; *our way was better than their way and the "us versus them" construct*, it was imperative to share all knowledge. Everywhere tools like patriotism were used to inculcate the masses with messages of intolerance and bigotry. Everywhere education was used to ensure conformity rather than foster enlightenment. The first thing that needed to be done was to do away with the evil forces of patriotism and greed and replace them with a sense of cosmic consciousness.

"My country is the world and my religion is to do good"
Thomas Paine

The Oracle knew that for growth to occur in a society it must be open to new information at all times, even if that information threatened existing beliefs. Social, spiritual, economic progress could only occur in open societies that embraced the search for truth and knowledge. If a society was truly to thrive there was no place for laws that suppressed the freedom to search for truth. There must be freedom of thought, freedom of speech, freedom of choice, and freedom of the press, if the search for truth is to occur. Society must then not fear change but embrace it, if real progress is to occur. There had to be a new globalization, not an economic one based on elitism, but a ideological one based on the knowledge that we are all one and that we will either sink or we will swim, but we will most definitely all do it together.

The Oracle had observed how mankind had abused his environment for profit and greed. He had seen how man had behaved like he was above Mother Nature and not part of it. He was disconnected. His religions had taught him that he was special, above other creatures of the earth. His sense of superiority had caused him to abuse nature, not to revere it. He did not realize that, when he abused another creature no matter how insignificant it appeared to be, he abused himself. He did not appreciate that by his actions he had driven many creatures to extinction, and that he would eventually drive himself to extinction. After all he was special. He misread the message in his religion. His religion had also told him to **"Love thy Neighbor as Thyself "**, but he did not understand. He did not realize that **his neighbor was not the guy next door, but was every creature on the planet.**

> *"The differences that separate mankind, pale in comparison*
> *to the similarities that unite us"*
> P. J. Morry 2012

The Oracle knew that the power of the cosmic consciousness would give man the knowledge and enlightenment to find his way. With weapons of truth and unconditional love for all things great and small, man would be able to connect to that cosmic energy and free himself from all the vicissitudes of ignorance that had chained him to his heavy loads of intolerance and greed. Knowing and fully understanding the concept that

"Love and Respect are something that you have to have to Get" would liberate him. Mankind would finally know the most important thing of all*: "The truth will set you free."*

Chapter XXIX

BACK ON EARTH

An unrecognizable, yet entirely familiar voice shook Bill out of his reverie and he instantly became aware of the chill that permeated his body. He was not sure if the voice came from inside his head or if it came on the wind. He felt his legs stiff beneath him. He felt something in his hand. When he looked in the direction of his hand he noticed that his arm and hand were semi translucent. He could see right through them. Slowly they started to re-materialized. In his hand was a beautiful flower that he had never seen before. The flower was shaped like a sphere with sixteen golden dots that were perfectly equidistant from each other. They were enmeshed in a web of silk that glowed from a blue light coming from its center. Strangely the darker it got outside the brighter the flower glowed. Finally, the flower turned into a vapor that invaded his nostrils and filled his lungs. He felt strange. He felt enlightened. Was he dreaming or was this real? He noticed it was getting dark; he had been there since early dawn. He felt light-headed, his body was shaking and he felt detached. Had he been possessed by a seeker that had filled him with enlightenment or was he weak from not eating that day? Had he travelled to all those places or had it been a dream? He would never know. That was a mystery he would happily leave unresolved, he had discovered all the truths that mattered. Armed with the sure and certain knowledge that he had learned all he needed, he stood, breathed deeply in the night air, smiled and began walking home with the light of truth guiding him. His footsteps were as sure and firm as his newfound resolve to teach his fellow beings all that he had learned. He was filled with hope, and confidence.

The next morning, he heard a rumor that the evening before a man had been seen walking on the beach just as it was getting dark. It was said that he had an iridescent glow as if he had a light inside him lighting his way. How was it possible that he had not crossed paths with this luminous man? Bill did not realize that, that man was himself. He looked out over the ocean. It was another beautiful day. It was the 24th of May. It was 8:00 am. The winds of change were blowing, first easterly then veering to southeasterly. The last vestiges of the low pressure system that had filled the night sky would soon be gone. A high pressure system was moving in. The sunbeams broke though a cloud pregnant with precipitation. Suddenly a light dusting of snowflakes briefly appeared. One exceptionally large flake caught Bills eye. It drifted towards the eastern window and just hung there above an English Red Rose for what seemed like three seconds as if struggling to delay its imminent demise. Finally it peacefully settled on the rose petal that anxiously awaited its arrival. It blended into the Rose and disappeared. Suddenly as if by magic the rose stiffened and a blush illuminated its petals. The snowflake had been transformed. Suddenly as if attracted by the rose's new glow, a sparrow settled on its branch and started to sing. A poem popped into Bill's head as if it had come straight from the sparrow's heart.

The Sparrow's Song

As I sat upon my deck one sunny day
A sparrow sang a song just feet away.
It jumped up on the table next to me,
And left me bathed in pure serenity.

The little bird did sing a song so fair,
It floated on the silent salty air.
As gentle waves did ripple on the shore,
I wished to part these soothing shores no more.

A New Day

Babbling brook, a sparrow's song
Morning mist, shadows long
Crimson clouds, salt filled air
Seagull's cry, rocking chair.

Thundering waves, foghorn wails,
Morning dew, furrowed sails,
Smell of coffee, sleep filled eyes
Radiant sunbeams fill the skies,

Morning shadows flee the sun
Another day has just begun.

Yesterday he had had the most incredible journey of enlightenment. In a few days, when the economic talks resumed, he would have the daunting task of spreading that message of enlightenment to the entire world in order to prevent worldwide economic collapse, with its subsequent mass starvation, violence and death. Today however is today and outside the sunbeams were bursting through the clouds, connecting earth and sky, filling him with wonder. He could see the magic circle of life resplendent before him as the snowflakes that had just fallen were again riding the sunbeams back into the heavens. He decided to go for another walk on the beach. His daughter Rebecca was home. He would take her with him. He loved his special place. He vowed never to leave it. This was his place of renewal. To him this place was the essence of God.

"Our search for truth will only be realized when we finally understand that there is no such thing as us and them. There is only we."
PJ Morry 2012

POSTSCRIPT

Life is a journey it is not a destination. Life is all about becoming, becoming the best that we can be, becoming aware of others and self. It is a search for truth and love. The journey is made by single steps, sometimes miniscule, sometimes gigantic. Success is not about money. It is not about how many things we acquire. It is not about how much power we have. Success is measured by what we have become and by what we are becoming. Success is steady progress towards a worthwhile goal. We can all be successful, if in our lives we make the worthwhile goal the search for truth and love.

No one is perfect. Perfection is unattainable. Some believe that it does not even exist. We all make mistakes, but what is important is that we all learn from our mistakes, and become more truthful. There is a quote by one of Americas leading TV personalities Dr. Phil that I dearly love. "You can't fix what you don't acknowledge." What an extremely powerful statement, for what it means is that we first must find truth before we can find peace and happiness. It means that if we lie to others we are also lying to ourselves. It is the first step of recovery; of moving from a victim to a survivor; of moving from a survivor to a healer, for a healer knows how to love, how to love without conditions. A healer is rich because he gives away his love.

If our planet is to survive with us in it, we must respect it. We must love everything in it without conditions. Only when we become one with nature, and not see ourselves above nature, and not see ourselves as special, will we truly be in harmony with the Universe. If mankind is to survive we must love everything that interacts with us unconditionally. The love must be unconditional for when we set conditions we establish a hierarchy.

We set up an "Us versus them" situation. We see ourselves as better than them. The "us versus them" mentality results in bigotry, indifference and intolerance. Hierarchies of rich and poor, have and have-nots, gay and straight, black and white, Christians and non Christians, Muslim and non Muslim are the source of all that is bad in the world. Because of these differences, the *"us versus them mentality* "we get misunderstanding, greed and envy. This in turn leads to war.

As we become loving, more accepting, more caring and more understanding of others in our journey we will shed the shackles of fear, suspicion and hatred.

Communication will become easier and with mutual respect we can start looking for solutions to the problems that plague mother earth. This journey must begin within each and every one of us. We cannot wait for the other guy to take the first steps. We must take the first steps, each one of us. We cannot fail to do so, in the complex world that exists today, with the type of weapons that exist today. The choice is clear, we have no choice. The money masters and the power seekers know how to exploit our weaknesses our feelings of fear and suspicion. They use those weaknesses to encourage greed. And the weapon they use to enslave us all is greed. The only weapon that is powerful enough to overcome the weapon of greed is the weapon of love. Love is all we need. Love is all there is. Love will free us all, but only if we give our love away.

**"The best thing about becoming is that
you never really get there."**

ACKNOWLEDGEMENTS

To my wife Jo, I wish to give special thanks for not only being a most loving mother and grandmother but for putting up with me for all these years. Life's journey is always challenging; change is inevitable, but not necessarily growth. The challenge both individually and collectively is to change and grow without growing apart. I owe my wife an eternal debt of gratitude for being there through all the changes, good and bad. Schnarch in his book Passionate Marriage calls marriage a "Mutually Sadistic Relationship", yet he says that passionate marriage is always possible if we can change and grow without necessarily compromising who we are. He calls this "Differentiation". Inherent in this concept is the idea that we must be able to accept the changes in our significant other without compromising who we are, or expecting our other to become something they are not; a daunting task to be sure. He describes a good marriage as two differentiated people in two different boats with the same destination. Both are interdependent, yet both are free to pursue a different path. Hopefully both spouses will remain in sync on the journey; interdependent but not co-dependent. The secret is daily frequent communication and mutual respect for not only our similarities but our differences. Our bumpy journey of change is just begun; our destination, so far, is still the same. We are still becoming.

I would be remiss if I did not give a special thanks to Pastor Mike McIntyre of Houston British Columbia Canada who tolerated my musings when he came to see me as a patient. Suffice it to say he helped me more than I helped him. His, was the hand on my shoulder in my time of greatest need.

To my father Bill Morry who was the most honest man I know I who a debt of gratitude for showing me the meaning of Integrity.

To my mother Pat Morry who possessed a profound belief that her fellow men were all equal in the eyes of God I owe everything. Thanks mom for making me help my neighbor, who was an old man, make his hay, when I would rather have been playing street hockey with my friends. Your example and unconditional love and respect for others have given me the ability to find my way in a complicated world.

For those who helped me edit this book and who read it in its development stage, and who offered their advice I owe special thanks. In the beginning this book may have sounded crazy to those who read it at that juncture, because it seemed I'm sure so disconnected and out there. For those who read it at that point in time and saw value in it I am eternally grateful. You know who you are, and it was your encouragement that kept me going when it would have been so easy to quit. I am eternally in your debt. Because of you I have completed a project, which I believe has worth even if it prompts only one person to *become*. Certainly the process has brought me inner peace, personal growth, clarity of thought, and a sense of fulfillment that are invaluable in my personal process of *becoming*. I thank you all from the bottom of my heart.

BIBLIOGRAPHY

1. Bruce Bagemihl; Biological Exuberance: Animal Sexuality and Natural diversity, St. Martin's Press, 1999; 0-312-19239-B

2. Max Harold (1909-02-16) "Biological Exuberance: Animal homosexuality and Natural diversity. The Advocate reprinted in Highbeam Encyclopedia. Retrieved 2007-09-10.

3. Gordon, Dr. Denis (10 April 2007). "Catalogue of Life reaches one million species." National Institute of Water and Atmospheric Research.

4. Calvin Reed "Gay Lib for the Animals" A new look at homosexuality in Nature. Volume 245 Issue 5 02/01/1999

5. "Same sex Behavior seen in nearly all Animals"; Review finds Science Daily.

6. "Same Sex Behavior seen in nearly all Animals" Physorg.com. 2009-06-16.

7. Levay, Simon 1996. Queer Science. The use and abuse of Research into Homosexuality. Cambridge, Mass. MIT Press p.207.

8. Bagemihl 1999 pp122-166

9. Joan Roughgarden, Evolution Rainbow; Diversity, gender and sexuality in nature and people. University of California Press, Berkley 2004; pp13-83.

10. Vasey, Paul L. (1995) Homosexual Behavior in Primates: A Review of Evidence and Theory; International Journal of Primateology 16: pp 173-204

11. Sommer, Volker and Paul L. Vasey (2006); Homosexual Behavior in Animals, an Evolutionary Perspective. Cambridge University Press, Cambridge. ISBN 0-521-86446-1

12. Douglas, Kate (Dec 7, 2009) "Homosexual Selection, The power of Same Sex Liaisons." New Scientist.

13. Gailey, D. A.; Hall J. C. "Behavior and Cytogenetics of fruitless in Drosophila Melanogasker. Different Courtship defects caused by Separated closely linked lesions:" Genetics the Genetic Society of America p121 (4) 773-785 PMC 1203660 PMID 2542123.

SUGGESTED READING

1. The Money Masters—YouTube

2. Zeitgeist The Movie—YouTube

3. The Shock Doctrine—Naomi Klein

4. LBJ The Mastermind of the JFK Assignation—Phillip E Nelson

5. The Art of Happiness—His Holiness the Dalai Lama and Howard c. Cutler M.D.

6. The Secret—Rhonda Byrne

7. The End of America—Naomi Wolf

8. In Plain Sight—YouTube

9. The Captain and the Kings—Taylor Caldwell

10. The Dollar Meltdown—Charles Goyette

11. 1984—George Orwell

12. The Elegant Universe—Brian Green

13. The Fabric of the Cosmos—Brian Green

14. Family of Secrets—Russ Baker

15. Healing Anger—His Holiness The Dalai Lama

16. The Hunger Games—Suzanne Collins

39. The Rise of the Fourth Reich:—Jim Marrs

40. The Elite Serial Killers of Lincoln JFK RFK and MLK—Robert Gaylon

41. The Case for Gold—Ron Paul

42. The Untold History of The United States—Oliver Stone / Peter Kuznick

43. The Naked Ape—Desmond Morris

44. Lament for an Ocean—Michael Harris

45. Rush to Judgment—Mark Lane

46. Plausible Denial—Mark Lane

47. Kill Zone—Craig Roberts

48. Girl on the Stairs—Barry Ernest

49. Cover Up: Behind the Iran Contra Affair—PBS Documentary

50. What is Money—Ron Paul Lecture Series (Three part documentary about money) on youtube

51. The CIA, Drug Trafficking and American Politics: The Political Economy of War—Documentary Youtube

52. Secrets of the CIA: Full Documentary—Youtube

53. Sex Crimes and The Vatican—BBC Documentary (youtube)

54. The Power of Nightmares: The rise of the Politics of Fear—TV Mini Series

55. State of Mind The Psychology of Control—www.infowars.com

56. Invisible Empire: A new World Order Defined—www.infowars.com